# SHINE
## THROUGH
# WISDOM

SADHVI SIDDHALI SHREE

Siddha Sangh Publications

SIDDHA SANGH PUBLICATIONS
9985 E. Hwy 56, Windom, Texas 75492
info@siddhayatan.org

www.siddhayatan.org
www.siddhalishree.com
www.shinethroughwisdom.com

ISBN - 0-9843854-6-0
ISBN - 978-0-9843854-6-1

Library of Congress Control Number - 2015944755

*Printed in the United States of America.*

**Disclaimer:** Please note that not all exercises, diet plans, or other suggestions, mentioned in this book are suitable for everyone. This book is not intended to replace the need for consultation with medical doctors and other professionals. Before changing any diet, exercise routine, or any other plans discussed in this book, seek appropriate professional medical advice to ensure it is acceptable for you. The author and publisher are not responsible for any problems arising from the use or misuse of the information, materials, demonstrations or references provided in this book. Results are not guaranteed.

*This book is dedicated to my master:*
*Acharya Shree Yogeesh.*
*Thank you for sharing your enlightened wisdom*
*with the world—may all Truth Seekers shine.*

# :: CONTENTS ::

# :: FOREWORD ::

Sadhvi Siddhali Shree is a very rare soul who is quickly advancing on her spiritual journey and will achieve her spiritual goal of shedding all of her karma—liberation. Not only is she fully dedicated to working hard on herself to grow spiritually, but also to establishing Siddhayatan Tirth and helping it flourish and expand worldwide. For all truth seekers, she is the best example of what hard work is to improve the self and society.

When Siddhali Shree first met me eleven years ago, I knew she had many hidden talents—communication, writing, music, technology, intelligence. Since then, I've tried to help her talents rise and shine. I truly don't have any words to describe how much she has worked on herself, how much she has done for her own spiritual progress, and how much she has helped other souls. She doesn't see it, but I do.

The truth is: when a disciple of a guru touches the highest peak of the spiritual journey, that day is the happiest day for the guru—it seems their life is complete. That is why I am very proud of Siddhali Shree for her personal growth and spiritual accomplishments. It is my wish that she continues to advance on the spiritual path, share her talents with the world, and spread the messages of the Tirthankaras and teachings from the ancient samanic tradition to every country.

*Shine Through Wisdom* is a unique book for you, the spiritual truth seeker. Every chapter is filled with gems, inspiration, and teachings that will help rejuvenate your life and awaken your soul. You will learn how to be healthy—physically, emotionally, mentally, and spiritually. You will learn hidden steps to help you advance on your path. The best thing is that you will learn how to fight the hurricanes and chaos in your mind and still be able to smile and be happy.

Though the language is simple, the wisdom is profound. It comes from Siddhali Shree's own self-realizations and deep spiritual experiences. Clear-cut and easy to understand, it is flavored with her witty and soulful nature as she challenges you to be shaken and stunned. When she asked me for the book's title, I meditated on what she had written and how it will impact you: you will *Shine Through Wisdom.*

My blessings to Sadhvi Siddhali Shree for creating this book for truth seekers and humanity. I always say that if you can change one person, you have changed the whole world. If by reading *Shine Through Wisdom* just one person totally changes, one hundred percent, then Sadhvi Siddhali Shree has already taken full advantage of her life and her mission is complete.

I don't have enough words to bless Siddhali Shree. I can only wish that she continues to make many, many books like this one so that all people worldwide will benefit from the true message of spirituality.

May this book deeply touch your life and ignite your soul.

Blessings,
Acharya Shree Yogeesh

# :: ACKNOWLEDGMENTS ::

**To my master Acharya Shree Yogeesh—**

Acharya Shree, you entered my life at a critical time in my spiritual journey when I was filled with darkness, illusion, confusion, and doubts. I was desperately seeking guidance, truth and the path to liberation. You promised to help me, and you have always kept your promise.

Because of you, I have transformed in unimaginable ways. No words can really express all the ways I have changed and transformed—I don't even think I can see all of it. After meeting you, studying your teachings, understanding them deeply, experiencing them first-hand, and being able to receive direct guidance, my spiritual journey was taken to new heights in such a short time. My soul is awakening. My soul is becoming free. All because of you.

There are no words to fully express the gratitude I feel for you. Just as you find it difficult to explain bliss and soul with words, the same difficulty applies to expressing my heartfelt thanks. But, I will try:

Thank you for believing in me, knowing the real me, guiding me, helping me remove my karma, paving the way for my soul to grow and awaken, teaching me, being my shining light, protecting me, challenging me, correcting me, pushing me, inspiring me, setting the best example for me, sharing the path and truth with me, and never giving up on me.

I also thank you for your endless compassion, kindness, love, time, energy, knowledge, generosity, vision, and presence. You are truly the best role model any soul can ask for. That is why I consider you my guru, my master, my father.

Needless to say, this book would not exist without you. By your grace, I have done my best to share what I have learned and understood from you over the last eleven years. I can only hope at least one soul will totally transform as a result of this book.

Thank you again from the bottom of my heart. I know that the only way I can express my infinite gratitude is by sharing your teachings to help others grow and awaken—I promise you I will—that is my whole purpose.

Thank you, again, for saving my soul.

**Anubhuti, Miles & Cody—**

You are my rock, my family. Thank you for your love, support, and encouragement. Special thanks to you, Cody, for helping me edit this book.

**To my parents—**

Mom, even though I only had thirteen years with you, I learned so much. You taught me to be independent, to always serve the community, and to be brave and never give up despite the challenges that come my way. Dad, I am eternally grateful to you. Thank you for being one of my greatest challenges in my early life. Because of you, I learned how to love and forgive myself. I also learned to follow my heart no matter what. Without the challenges, I would have never questioned how to find happiness or begin my search for truth.

# :: INTRODUCTION ::

When I turned five years old, Grandma gave me the gift of piano lessons. For seven years, every Wednesday at three pm I walked down the block to learn from an elderly piano teacher, Ms. Anderson. There were days I would walk to Ms. Anderson's home feeling guilty, because I didn't practice any of the lessons assigned. On other days, I was so proud of what I had accomplished that I would run to her home so I could show her that I could play. When I was five, I wanted to be the best piano player in the whole wide world. I didn't like it when I experienced frustration, was overwhelmed, felt I couldn't advance, had trouble getting my techniques right, got hurt for not doing a good job, and I wanted to give up on myself because I just couldn't do it. Despite my inner battle and

9

wanting to give up many times (doesn't TV sound better than practicing piano for a five-year-old, anyways?), I continued practicing. "Work (or practice) before pleasure," Grandma would always tell me as she turned off the TV. After thousands of hours of learning and practicing piano over the years, I started to write my own spiritual music when I was twenty-four. If I hadn't put in the effort, I wouldn't be able to play piano or write music today. I am grateful to my practices.

You are reading this book because either you are interested in becoming spiritual or you want to be even more spiritual. Either way, you're awesome! The time is now for you to connect deeply with your true self, your soul. Don't waste your time. Don't waste your life. Be spiritual, be free—now. Spiritual practices will take you higher and lead you to freedom.

There are many reasons why you might be interested in becoming a more spiritual you. Maybe at this point in your life you are feeling lost, confused, frustrated, want to discover who you are but don't know how, doubt yourself, are tired of religion, tired of believing in something without having any experiences, living with guilt, living in fear, having low energy, constantly thinking negatively, feeling upset that you haven't found your passions or purpose, not believing in yourself, or tired of reading about spirituality and not feeling like you are growing or changing or experiencing all those cool spiritual things others talk about. Maybe, you recently heard about spirituality and are simply curious about it all. Whether you identify with some or all of these things, after going through this book and doing the daily practices, you will be more spiritual than you ever have been before. That's a pretty bold statement, but I know from experience that when you do any practice wholeheartedly, with the understanding of why it is important, its benefits, and actually doing it because you know it will make you better, transformation happens.

There are two common ways to approach spirituality: taking baby steps and growing slowly but steadily, or, taking leaps by learning too much too quickly, then realizing later you need to take baby steps. It's very easy to want to learn all aspects of spirituality, from karma, yoga, soul awakening, meditation, reincarnation, higher consciousness, chakras, enlightenment, liberation and so on. However, I always say, keep spirituality simple. When your path is simple, it's easier to progress. When your path becomes complicated from accumulating too much knowledge, you end up being scattered and going backwards instead of forward. You need to grow and move forward.

I recently met a man at Siddhayatan Spiritual Retreat, where I live and teach, who had a lot of knowledge on different areas of spirituality. When he came to visit, he brought a lot of books with him and had a lot of questions on how to grow spiritually, including how to become enlightened. It was interesting to see how someone with so much book knowledge on a variety of topics did not reflect, in his thoughts, actions, and speech, all that he had been reading about for years. He didn't practice, so he didn't grow. He was full of ego and believed he knew everything. Knowledge doesn't take you anywhere. Practice and humbleness leads you to yourself. What is the point of collecting knowledge anyways? Spirituality means to empty yourself of all negativities and everything you've collected. Collecting information is useless to the soul. Information belongs to the mind. Spirituality means to burn all of that information away. Emptiness belongs to your soul. When you are empty, you have nothing tying you down. You are truly free.

From the Tattvarth Sutra, a book from the ancient Jain System, the very first line is: *Samyag darshan, gyan, charitrani moksh margah.* **Right vision, right knowledge, and right conduct are the path to liberation.** This is all you need to know and practice. Ever. These are the three jewels that will lead you to your freedom. This one line is the core of your spirituality. It's simple, yet very deep. It requires one thing: practice.

To have right vision means you see Truth for what it absolutely is. There is not a single drop of influence from your mind, ego, emotions, beliefs, ideologies, religion, culture, people, and other forms of pollution. You see things clearly and have absolute crystal clarity. There are no clouds of illusion covering your perceptions.

To have right knowing means you know the Truth. You know all things through soul-realization. Soul has infinite power and knowing, and through right knowing, you know all Truth. This has nothing to do with bachelor, master or doctorate degrees, book knowledge, scriptural knowledge, or any other type of collected knowledge. Once you have removed all knowledge and bits of information from your mind, you will have access to your soul's knowing.

To have right conduct means you live in Truth and are 100% nonviolent in your behavior. You achieve right conduct by being nonviolent in your thoughts, actions and speech. Where there is violence, spirituality is far away from you. Not even a single negative thought or emotion can be inside you. When you are nonviolent within yourself, all actions are nonviolent.

By achieving these three jewels, you will achieve liberation. This means your soul has reached its highest state of consciousness. You no longer experience pain or suffering. You are also free from the cycle of birth and death. You experience eternal bliss.

Now you know the three jewels—the three keys—that will lead you to your soul's bliss. You also know that knowing this simple statement means nothing, unless you practice and improve yourself. Practice is what removes dirt from the soul. Reading about it doesn't.

## WHO ARE YOU?

Whether you are new to spirituality or not, it is always good to learn or be reminded about who you really are. You are soul. What that means is you are a pure, innocent, and divine being. Your qualities are only the best. You are like a light. You are shapeless, formless, and timeless. The essence of you is total knowing and aliveness. Directly, *appa so paramappa*. You are God and God is you.

Being spiritual means to dedicate your life to learning more about your true self, transforming your lower qualities into higher qualities, awakening your soul, removing anything that covers your soul, such as karma, and learning to live from this purest part of you. Being spiritual means to live nonviolently, to be compassionate, calm, peaceful, understanding, nonjudgmental, without hatred, and to feel oneness and unconditional love with all living beings (not just limited to your family or friends).

To be spiritual and to embody your true essence, you have to go beyond and dissolve all that you have believed yourself to be. Many people and things, both positive and negative, have influenced you to become who you are today. I call them the pollutants that cover your soul. The pollution is like clouds that cover the sun. You are the sun. The clouds are not you. As you begin to know you are not the clouds and that you are the sun, you become more and more spiritual, and awakened.

If you look into a baby's eyes, you see purity and innocence. You see their divinity. Babies are born with no mind. The mind and its ideologies are acquired, learned, collected and then over time become corrupted. You first learn how to think, believe, speak and act from your caretakers, maybe your parents or grandparents. The way they raised you was based on their perceptions of the world, their culture, their religious beliefs, their positive/negative habits, what their interpretation of life is, and their expectations from society. Remember, the real you is not what you have been given. You have been given a body, a name, your mind, an education, belief system, etc. Being spiritual means to get to know who you were as a baby, the moment before you were born and entered this world. That is why spirituality is a backwards journey. You were alive in the womb, right? That is the direction in which you need to go if you want to be more spiritual. You need to discover and get to know the real you. The real you—the you not tainted by the world or the people of it.

I know. I know. You might think it is impossible to remember that far back. "Memories from the womb? Really? You're crazy, Sadhvi Siddhali Shree." Remember, your soul knows all things and holds all memories. You can reconnect to those precious moments through concentration, relaxation, and deep meditation. Nothing is lost. When you learn to know who you really are, and live from the pure, innocent, and divine you, then you will be unaffected by pain and suffering. There is a saying, "The spiritual path lies in the purest-of-the-pure heart." Don't think it is impossible to be spiritual and live from your true self. Nothing is impossible. Practice is what helps you get there.

The pollution, or dirt, that covers and disturbs your soul, unfortunately, has great strength. Even though soul knows everything and has infinite power, it is presently weak and asleep. It has been in the grip of the pollution for so long and has begun to believe those lies. When the soul begins to become curious about spirituality, it already shows it is beginning to wake up—and that's a BIG thing. The main pollution that covers your soul is **Karma**.

Karmas are like dust particles that stick to your soul and cover it. Each and every moment we are collecting good or bad karmic particles based on our intentions, thoughts, actions, and speech. Some karma might be as light as dust and easily removed. Some might be as hard as concrete, which requires great strength to remove. Our intention creates the degree, or amount, that we collect—lots of dust or lots of concrete. Being spiritual means to dedicate your life to stopping the collection of karma and burning the karma you already have, removing the clouds of illusion covering your soul. When you burn all of your karma, you attain the three jewels. You attain liberation.

Other examples of pollution that take us away from our soulful nature come from our parents, guilt, pressures of societal success, anger, the need to be perfect and fit in, jealousy, religious beliefs, cultural beliefs, deceit, entertainment, negative peer influences, addictions and habits, eating meat, feeling like a failure, and much more. Any time you begin to think, speak, and act negatively towards yourself or others, your soul becomes weaker and weaker. It's not a thin layer of pollution that covers your soul. The layers are thick and dense. It's like trying to see the moonlight during an intense thunderstorm, a hurricane, and a tornado happening all at once. The moon is there, but because of the thick clouds and extremely bad weather, it's difficult to see and believe it exists.

The karmic pollution affects us emotionally, mentally, physically, and spiritually. They stay embedded in our body and mind as toxins. Until we begin to remove the pollution, the karma, the toxins, will always cover our nature. We have to remove the pollution in order to know our soul. To be spiritual means to be a karma-pollution remover.

**How to remove the pollution is what this book is about.**

There are different practical ways to remove the karma, toxins, and pollution that cover your soul. For the next thirty-one days, I will share with you different types of teachings and sadhana. Sadhana means spiritual practices specifically intended to remove karma (pollution) from your soul. Some of these include exercises, writing assignments, yoga postures, breathing techniques, concentration techniques, mantras, meditations, chakra activation, self-healing, and other tips and secrets I have learned on my path and that have helped me. I will also share with you why it is important, as well as stories and examples from my own life.

## My Story

One day in September 2001, I was not paying attention during my British Literature class and was writing away in my notebook. I had tuned out my high school teacher and classmates. The entire period I was writing my thoughts and feelings. It was the last class of the day and once the school bell rang, my teacher came over to me and started to read what I had written. I didn't like that very much, but I didn't have a choice. One of the lines written was, "I just want this world to end." It wasn't a suicide note, even though I had tried to do that a few times. I was tired of my current world. The one that was filled with pain, loneliness, hate, anger, feeling lost and confused. My world of suffering.

My mom had died when I was thirteen, after a five-month battle with cancer. One month after her death, my dad had my grandma and brother (whom I'd lived with my entire life) leave my home, as they were both unrelated to him. I felt an extreme loss. And soon after, my dad remarried. I'm sure you can imagine that I was not happy at all—mostly angry, feeling betrayed, alone, feeling unimportant, hurt, depressed, and the list can go on. Despite my painful experiences, throughout high school I considered myself an eternal optimist—hurt yet hopeful.

At this particular moment in my high school classroom, I was desperately seeking a turning point in my life. I wanted some kind of change, some kind of true happiness, something good—a switch that could make my dark world full of light. My English teacher passed on my note to my high school counselor. After an introduction and some superficial discussion, she asked me one question that ultimately changed my life. She asked, "Do you love yourself?" My answer was, "No. That sounds selfish." That question struck me. It made me think. I got quiet. Then I asked myself one question, "If I were to love myself, who am I supposed to love?" I had no answer for that. Then I asked myself the main question that jump-starts most spiritual journeys: "Who am I?"

For the rest of my senior year, I was very interested in reading self-help books. I wanted to know more and more about myself. I wanted to let go of any pain and suffering I was holding on to. I wanted to be happy. I wanted to be free. I wanted to love myself to the fullest.

The summer after I graduated, I started doing yoga and learning how to meditate. I had never felt so free in my entire life. I jumped heavily into reading Eastern spirituality. I had never heard about soul, or karma, and knowing the true self. I was fascinated and very curious. Even though I was raised Catholic and went to Catholic elementary and high school, I felt an inner pull to start moving my life towards learning more and more about soul. I felt I had been missing out on good stuff my entire life.

After some time, I eventually joined a Hindu group and immersed myself in the teachings, techniques, and their forms of yoga and meditation. It felt good for a while, but afterwards I started to see it wasn't the path for me. I had a lot of spiritual questions that their teachings and teachers couldn't answer. Their actions were in contradiction to what they were teaching. I also felt they didn't know or see my spiritual potential wanting to be unleashed. I wanted to be spiritual, but realized I needed a living master to help me.

When I was twenty years old, I came into contact with my guru, Acharya Shree Yogeesh, who is an enlightened master. A guru means "one who dispels darkness." After meeting Acharya Shree, my path and spirituality became very clear. It wasn't easy studying under him at first, but I was eager to learn. I was very impatient and wanted to see results right away. I was very goal-oriented. I remember he told me on the day I first met him, "Slow and steady wins the race. I can help you, but you need to have patience. I want you to know and understand these teachings deeply. You need right guidance. When you understand the teachings and practice them, you will achieve what you are seeking." Liberation.

Four months after I met Acharya Shree, I received the worst phone call of my life—I was getting deployed to Iraq. I thought to myself, "For the first time I'm happy, I found my spiritual teacher, and now I'm being blocked from my path." I was away from home for a total of sixteen months. I was deployed to Tikrit, Iraq, as an Army Combat Medic. I was part of convoys that were often driven on roads filled with Improvised Explosive Devices (IEDs). If something bad were to happen, it would be my duty to help any patient.

Coming back home was not an easy adjustment. Even though I did my best to do my mantras and meditations in a war zone, I still lost myself. Deep inside, I knew I was spiritual. I knew I had this voice inside me still. It was just under a lot of thick clouds. I wanted to desperately find myself again and to be spiritual in all aspects of my life. I went back to the ashram and continued to learn from Acharya Shree. I learned different techniques to help me find myself again. After four to six months of intense practice, I was back to myself, and even more driven towards spirituality than before. It was finally my time to start training to become a monk.

Eventually, I will write my memoir about these major life experiences and how I overcame all of them. For now, I want to briefly share with you that I had a painful past. It was dark and scary, but with time, spiritual practices, understanding, and right guidance, I was able to find myself. Throughout this book, you'll see how we are similar. I'll also share with you my mistakes, misconceptions, and other things I wish I would've known. This way you don't have to make the same mistakes I did or be misled.

Every day I continue working on myself. Every day, I learn something new. Every day, I live by my soul more and more. I wish the same for you. Remember, I'm like you: a seeker, a spiritual person who wants to be free.

*Shine Through Wisdom* is my chance to spend time with you each and every day to help you grow, remove the karma and pollution that blocks you from your soul, help you move beyond any pain and suffering in your life, and share with you how you can transform spiritually and awaken.

When you make a commitment to yourself that for the next thirty-one days you will practice what is being suggested, you will see the positive results after the period is over. If you don't see it, others will. That's what usually happens on the path — we tend to not see our own transformation. Once we begin to hear the comments from others, that's when we believe it. "Wow, you've changed. Something is different about you. You seem more calm and peaceful. Wow! You're glowing. You seem so happy." Remember, when you do anything wholeheartedly, without tension or expectation, you let go of the old and open up space for the new, real you to shine through.

It's your time now to remove the clouds of pollution and illusion that cover your beautiful, shining, unconditionally loving, pure, innocent, and blissful self. It's your time to move the needle in your life. I can't wait for you to meet the real you!

Before we get started, I want to share with you how you can get the most out of this practical book. First, read one day's section and do the activity assigned each and every day. It is better not to skip ahead or pick and choose what you'd like to do. I'm challenging you to remove layers of pollution. Sometimes it might be scary and you might be a little resistant or fearful (anytime the mind feels threatened it will try to block you). Remind yourself that you want to grow, transform, and be spiritual and you are willing to do whatever it takes to get there. No. Matter. What.

Get a journal that is dedicated to your activities from this book. I include many reflective questions that I would like you to explore and answer. What you put in, you will get out. The more honest, raw, and vulnerable you answer the questions, the more you benefit. Keep your journal in a safe and secret spot, this way you do not have to worry about someone else finding and reading it.

Stay motivated. One of the pollutions to the soul is laziness. It's easy to say, "It's okay if I miss today, there is still tomorrow, and I can continue where I left off." Remember, your soul has been waiting years to start doing these practices. It wants to remove the pollution now. It wants to be happy and free now. Don't let it wait an extra day!

The goal of this book is to help you become spiritual by teaching you how you can remove all of your pollution. My wish for you is to shine brightly like the sun, with no clouds covering it.

Practice. Practice. Practice.

Your freedom is near.

# :: CONFESSION ::

There are heavy chains that keep ourselves down and far away from feeling and being free. And of course, we want freedom. These chains are in the form of secrets, habits, regrets, fears, mistakes, judgments, resentment, negative emotions like anger, jealousy, greediness, and hatred towards ourselves and others. When you hold on to these negativities in your heart, it truly weighs you down. Holding on to these chains can cause you great stress, sickness, anxiety, pain in the body, feeling overwhelmed and frustrated, upset at yourself, guilty, and similar feelings. Maybe you are able to play it off with fake smiles and hide it from others and no one knows, but you know the truth. You cannot hide from yourself. As an aspiring spiritual person, you need to purify yourself. You need a clean slate. You need to let go. You need to be free. One way to do that is through confession. Confession is the act of releasing anything you are holding on to that makes you feel negative, guilty, regretful, and dark.

Before you can dive deeply into the future spiritual practices I will give you, you need to be at a point where you are willing to change because you've identified the negative things you no longer want to be a part of you. You have to face yourself head on. It takes courage and bravery, but I know you have these qualities. You're tired of being tired. You're tired of feeling lost or unhappy or feeling you're not getting anywhere. By confessing everything you've done, experienced, felt, or thought towards yourself and others, you will be amazed how much relief and how much lighter you will feel. Can you imagine your life with all those negativities and their weight removed? Bliss is on the other side, my friend.

I remember the first time I confessed to Acharya Shree everything I had been carrying inside. In my mind, I was the worst person on earth. I was mad at myself for my thoughts and negative feelings, and even harder on myself because I was leading a spiritual and nonviolent life as a monk. I'm human — I was weak, and I messed up — a lot. Of course on the outside no one knew what I was feeling or thinking. What made it worse is that people looked up to me as their role model, and there I was failing all over the place. Regardless of what I was experiencing, I was so tired of not facing it and being controlled by my negativities. By not facing it, it had more control and power over my soul. My purpose is to strengthen my soul and free myself from the chains of karma, yet they were still controlling me. I remember I asked Acharya Shree if I could confess to him. I struggled how to start. I was afraid, embarrassed, mad, and ashamed. I knew that Acharya Shree was someone that I could trust. He knows how strong ignorance and karma can be and how they cloud the soul—he knows the chains. All his teachings are meant to free us from those chains. So after talking superficially for a few minutes, trying to beat around the bush, feeling and seeing my heart's pulse going fast, I took a deep breath, and said, "Okay. I already know you know everything that is going on inside of me, but I'll say it now." After my list of negative feelings, thoughts, and actions were released, which took me at least an hour to say, I felt so vulnerable, so raw, yet so free. Finally, all those things I was carrying inside were released—things I was hanging on to for years that had control over me or felt guilty about. But finally, I had a clean slate and my soul was in control. There was freedom in my confession.

There are a few ways to confess. My first advice is, be careful who you tell all these things to. We live in a society of judgment, backstabbing, and gossip, so I advise not to tell friends or family or coworkers. My suggestion is to either tell a spiritual teacher or tell nature, like a tree, flower, bird, or dog. Both work. Both will listen, not judge and help you feel peaceful. Of course it will be awkward, but that's normal. The point is, you'll get it out. And who knows, as soon as you feel the relief, the spiritual teacher or nature might give you some advice.

You can also write everything you want to confess and let go of. Then read it out loud in privacy. Then carefully burn the piece(s) of paper. All of your negative past will have no power over you anymore.

If it helps and if you feel comfortable, you can email me your confession at confession@siddhalishree.com. I will be the only one to read these emails — I promise — this way it is out of your system, you feel safe, you won't be judged, and you know you are telling someone.

Or you can send me what you write down directly. Address it to:

Sadhvi Siddhali Shree
Shine Through Wisdom: Day 1
9985 E Hwy 56
Windom, TX 75492

You can do it anonymously from a fake email or mailing address, as long as it is out of you, that makes me happy and proud of you.

There's a series of books called *Post-Secret* and you can view many entries at http://www.postsecret.com to get an idea of the secrets people have been carrying inside, that they finally released. Caution! Warning! Disclaimer! Some secrets can be really intense when you read them, but don't judge others. Remember, you have your own. Have the courage, like them, to release it.

By confessing, you will create awareness not to think, say, or do those things again, you will reduce the strengths of any addiction or habits, you will create self-awareness which helps you prevent future chains, you will have peace of mind, and you will have a new start.

ACTIVITY: Confess.

Today, spend some time reflecting on anything and everything you know deep down inside you that has been bothering you or holding you down. It could be emotions, thoughts, actions, things you've done, said, regret, have kept a secret, etc. It will be scary to write it all down and to face it, but remind yourself you will no longer have these chains

Sadhvi Siddhali Shree

holding you.

It's time to let go. No more chains. Fly.

# :: NONVIOLENCE ::

Nonviolence means to not hurt, harm, or kill any living being (including yourself) through your thoughts, actions and speech, to not encourage others to be violent (towards themselves and others), and not appreciate those who are violent. When you live a nonviolent life, you no longer collect any karmic pollution to cover your soul. Nonviolence is the key to help you achieve the third jewel, right conduct.

When I first met Acharya Shree Yogeesh at his ashram, he didn't teach me yoga, meditation, or breathing techniques or the advanced, complex, and complicated spiritual teachings I was secretly desiring and craving. I remember he said, "Today, I'm going to teach you about nonviolence. You need to know and understand this principle fully." In my mind, I was disappointed. I wanted the *good stuff*, like learning how to be *super* spiritual, to connect with my past lives, or maybe to learn how to read minds. But no, it was nonviolence. It makes me laugh now how much I didn't know back then, when I believed I knew a lot. I didn't realize then that nonviolence is the heart —the treasure, the light, the key—of the spiritual path. When you master nonviolent living, freedom is there. Even now, over eleven years later, he continues to teach me about nonviolence.

**Nonviolence is the first step of spirituality.** I want to share this teaching with you first, like Acharya Shree did with me. Meditation, yoga, and other pollution-removing techniques that I will share with you soon are tools to help you remove karma that you have already collected. Learning nonviolence now helps you prevent karma collection. If you learn how to prevent something, then you do not have to face any of the negative consequences. That's why I do not support much research for the cure to cancer, even though my mom died of it. I'd rather support research to find the cause and prevention of it. If you know the cause and how to prevent it, then there's no need for a cure. In the same way, if you master nonviolence and stop covering your soul with pollution, it isn't important to learn pollution-removing techniques.

Violence comes in two forms: visible and invisible. The

visible violence includes wars, killing, or harming humans and non-humans, arguments, physical fighting, hunting, slaughtering animals, domestic violence, rape and sexual abuse, torture, and the list can go on and on. Even though this violence is terrible, the worst kind of violence is the invisible one.

Invisible violence is the most dangerous because it dominates our thoughts. A person can appear calm and mellow to the outside world, but may have violent thoughts like thinking bad or low about themselves, self-hate, judging others, jealousy, or maybe they are having very violent thoughts like hurting or killing someone. Internal violence is easy to remain hidden behind gentle eyes and a smile. Humans are such great actors.

That's why if we want to be spiritual and be nonviolent and see nonviolence and peace reflected in our planet, we need to work on our inner violence first. In my opinion, self-violence is the most evil of them all.

Self-violence means you think negatively about yourself, live in constant fear, anger, jealousy, deceitfulness, greediness or have an arrogant and huge ego. Self-violence includes hating yourself, thinking you are not smart, thinking you are not beautiful, thinking you are not good enough, thinking you do not matter, or that you don't deserve anything good in life, thinking you are a failure. When immersing yourself in such violent and negative thoughts, all day, every day, your soul becomes weaker and weaker.

Acharya Shree says the main terrorists that exist today live inside our minds. We can be so mean and cruel as we torture ourselves. The soul does not like this heavy pollution at all. The soul wants to be free. Remember, you are not your mind, thoughts, feelings or body. You are soul — pure, innocent and divine.

When you become nonviolent in your thoughts towards yourself, you automatically become nonviolent in your thoughts towards others. When your thoughts are pure and divine, your speech and actions will reflect nonviolence too. That is why all change starts with you.

To transform and grow spiritually, dissolve your inner violence by eliminating all negative and violent thoughts towards yourself and others. To help you achieve nonviolent thinking, change the words you use.

You would think to change your thoughts first before changing the way you speak, but actually the opposite is true. When you are cautious in how and what you speak to others and to yourself out loud, you already have increased your awareness towards nonviolent thinking. It's easier to control your speech than your thoughts. But once you master this, your thoughts will change automatically.

We will touch on nonviolence through the entire book so you learn more and more how to create that lifestyle and integrate it into your life.

Activity: Reflect and write.

In your journal today, reflect and describe how you've been violent in your thoughts, actions, and speech (towards yourself and others). What can you do daily to help yourself become aware of shifting from violence to nonviolence?

# :: MEDITATION ::

Meditation, in the deepest, truest sense, means to be in tune with your soul. This requires you to go beyond your body, mind, and thoughts. Meditation, when you are able to be in that state fully, is your greatest ally when it comes to burning your karma. When you are in deep meditation, your karma burns and dissolves. All those clouds begin to move away from your soul very quickly. The reason is because in the state of meditation you are no longer identified with yourself, your surroundings, your mind, or even your body. In meditation, you feel emptiness, nothingness, and everythingness. It's a very peaceful, blissful state. I'm referring to the highest states of meditation. The highest state of meditation is actually the real you.

Today in society, meditation is known as an act. Meditation is considered something you need to learn and *do*. It already suggests that meditation is separate from you. The reality is: meditation is you. Meditation is your nature. Meditation is the state of being where you are with your soul. Unfortunately, since meditation is taught to be separate from you and it is something that you must do, the common tools to teach meditation are incorrect. For example, a lot of meditation teachers and eastern schools of thought focus on controlling the mind.

The more you control the mind, the farther and farther you get away from being in tune yourself. The reason is this: by controlling your thoughts and mind (which is impossible) you create tension in the body. As soon as there is tension in the body, the state of meditation cannot happen. When you learn to relax and let go, meditation can happen. The more you control something, the farther and farther peace is away from you. Have you noticed controlling people? Nothing is really in their control since they live in a constant state of fear. Meditation happens when you are present, in the flow, and away from identifying with your body, mind, and thoughts. And since you cannot control the mind, how can meditation happen?

Meditation happens when you learn how to bypass the mind. Instead of trying to control it, learn not to pay attention to it. Acharya Shree says, "One of the laws of the universe is: the more you pay attention to something, the stronger it becomes." So if you are trying to relax and be in meditation and you are constantly aware of your thoughts and telling your mind to "be quiet" then, of course, it is not going to become quiet. Why? You're paying attention to it. When you learn to bypass your mind and thoughts and not pay attention to it, you will start entering the states of meditation.

It's like a child who is at home doing her homework at the kitchen table. She knows the television is on and she can hear it, but she is so focused on her homework that whatever is on the television is not affecting her. In the same way, you need to focus on your soul, connecting to stillness, peace, tranquility, serenity, and calmness inside you versus paying attention to that chatter box of mind.

I was fifteen years old when I first attempted meditation. My uncle was beginning to practice meditation at that time and so he was excited to share with me what he had learned. When I left his apartment, he gave me a black meditation pillow. As soon as I got home, I sat on the pillow and followed his instructions. I closed my eyes. Took a deep breath. And rolled my eyes up to a point between the eyebrows. I sat there for two minutes trying to figure out how to meditate. My mind was racing, "Am I doing this right? My eyeballs hurt. Do I have homework due on Monday? I wonder if I can read minds after this meditation session." After the two minutes, I gave up and grabbed a bowl of cereal. I told myself, meditation wasn't for me.

Three years later, I attempted meditation again. I was at a yoga studio where their focus was more on promoting spirituality versus strictly yoga postures. It was a relaxing environment. I had hope that I could find myself through meditation. I grabbed a meditation pillow and sat on the floor cross-legged. I touched my index finger and thumb together, resting my hands on my knees. The teacher asked me to close my eyes, take a deep breath, and look at the point between my eyebrows. Just like my uncle had told me before. I followed the instructions again. Desperate to figure out meditation, I focused very hard. I focused so hard I gave myself a headache.

Who gives themselves a headache when they are learning meditation? Of course that would be me. The thing is, I didn't give up. At that time in my life I was very curious about learning who I really was, and I knew that meditation was the way. People have been using meditation for thousands of years, seeking to discover themselves. I had to keep giving it a chance. Once I learned to let go, meditation began to happen. I felt the peace, warmth, and love in my heart. Hey, that was the real me.

With over twelve years of meditation experience, I'm very happy to tell you that I have changed drastically as a result of entering those deep states of meditation. I've gained understanding, insight, realizations, and most important, have had beautiful moments of connecting with my true self, the soul. Entering these deep states doesn't happen overnight. It takes a lot of time and *effort*. If you do not give yourself the time to be in meditation, how do you expect to be in tune with yourself?

The greatest benefit of being in meditation is that you are connected with the real you. The second benefit is that you begin to burn your karma. By being in a relaxed state and not having any tension in your body and mind, the pollution surrounding your soul automatically begins to loosen up. As it loosens, the karma's grip on you becomes less and less. The less grip karma has on you, the freer you become. Tension and stress attract karma. Relaxation releases it. Meditation is the state of total relaxation. Other benefits of being in meditation are clarity, peace, self-discovery, reduced high blood pressure, forgiveness, learning to be in the present moment, releasing anger and negativities, reduced stress, increased intuition and intelligence, improved concentration power, and mental/

emotional healing.

Meditation is a vast subject. I will continue to go deeper on meditation throughout your thirty-one days. This way you have a solid understanding of what meditation is and you have the opportunity to be in it.

ACTIVITY: Be in meditation for ten minutes.

Set aside time today. Find a quiet place in your house or out in nature. Sit comfortably with your spine straight. Close your eyes. Do seven deep breaths—inhaling and exhaling slowly. Relax and let go. If your mind gets in the way, don't pay attention to it or acknowledge it. Feel the peace. Feel the calmness. You are there.

# :: MANTRAS ::

Mantras are divine sounds that create colorful electricity and energy so that they heal you mentally, emotionally, physically and spiritually. They are carefully designed by masters who know the connection between syllables, sound, and energy. They know that through reciting certain syllable and sound combinations, a particular energy is created to produce certain results. Real mantras come from the natural and most ancient language Prakrit. Some mantras are also in Sanskrit, which is refined Prakrit.

There are many mantras out there—universal, religious, and fake. In this book, we will focus on the universal mantras. Fake ones don't get you results. Religious ones keep you in the small box. Universal ones are simply liberating. And we want you to be liberated from your karma, right?

What is great about universal mantras is that they can be recited by any and every one regardless of faith, religion, culture, etc. If you might be hesitant about reciting mantras because they are not familiar to you and seem religious in nature, don't be. There is a science to reciting these sounds and they will help you, free you.

Mantras are one of the best tools to help you remove your karmic pollution. There are no mantras for karma removal, but by reciting mantras your karma can be removed. That sounds contradictory. Let me explain.

Our souls are covered by karmic particles and the way to remove the pollution is through burning the karma. It is not easy to burn the karma. Through practice, patience, and persistence it can be removed. In order to burn karma, you have to create a fire inside to burn off all those particles. Meditation is the main karma burner, because when you are able to fully relax, meditation creates an intense fire and releases the karma. Mantras are a tool to help you go into meditation, which then leads to the possibility of karma burning. Mantras themselves do not burn the karma. Instead, they create the situation for it to happen. There are no syllable and sound combinations to burn off karma. All karma needs to give you a result somehow. If burning karma were as easy as reciting special sounds a certain number of times, we would all be happy, blissful, enlightened, and liberated by now. But no, we see suffering around the world and we suffer too. Karma burning is not that easy. Being in meditation is not that easy. Anything that seems too easy on the spiritual path shows you it is not real.

The benefits of mantras are many. The mantras create electricity that can protect you from negative people, things, situations, and evil; increase intellect, focus, and concentration; develop intuition; overcome depression, anxiety and fears; activate your chakras; emotional healing; create high-level spiritual energy for advancement, and much more. Most important, they help your mind focus on something while you enter deep meditation and connect to the soul.

A very important aspect of mantras is that they must be pronounced correctly in order to produce the right electricity and energy. When a mantra is pronounced incorrectly, even though your intention is good, it can bring you negative results. You also have to be careful from whom you learn. One day, one of Acharya Shree's disciples was asking me about Oprah and Deepak Chopra's 21-Day Meditation Experience and showed me a video as a reference to her question. During

47

the video, Deepak was teaching a mantra that included the word *Hum*. There is no seed mantra with the sound "hum" using an "mmm" sound. There is a seed mantra that is spelled Ham, but sounds like "hung." The "m," according to Sanskrit, is supposed to be pronounced with an "ng" sound. Again, if any mantra is pronounced incorrectly, regardless of intention, it can bring opposite or negative results. Be careful who you learn from. I want you to move forward on your journey with right guidance. Not go the other way!

Because correct pronunciation is critical, you can visit http://shinethroughwisdom.com/mantras to download free mp3s that I have created for you to listen, study and practice to. I learned directly from Acharya Shree Yogeesh the correct pronunciation. So, you are set!

There are two main ways to recite mantras. You can recite them out loud, like a chant. Or, you can recite them repeatedly, mentally. Both work. However, if you want to generate more electricity, then recite them out loud. The most important thing with mantras is that you should recite them wholeheartedly without expectation. The deeper you go into the mantra, the more your mind and body relax, thus creating chances for you to jump into meditation.

When going deep into the mantra, you might enter

meditation. You will be connected and totally in tune with your soul. Your awareness is with your soul. Yet, at the same time, in the far distance, you might *hear your mind* still repeating the mantra. The biggest difference is that you are not paying attention to the mind because you have bypassed it. You are focused on the soul.

It may feel odd to keep repeating the same words over and over and over again. In the beginning you might feel restless, think it is useless, or get easily bored. These are normal. The reason is that your mind is not used to focusing on one thing over and over again. The mind doesn't want you to grow spiritually, because the mind wants to continue ruling over, controlling, and dominating your life. With time and practice, your mind will begin to cooperate with you. The mind will eventually know that you are super serious and will give you that space to enter meditation. Until then it will bother and distract you. Don't pay attention to it. Bypass it. Focus on the mantra.

I remember when I first became a monk, Acharya Shree had increased my sadhana from my daily practice of thirty minutes pre-monkhood to three hours. My mind was used to reciting mantras for thirty minutes, but not used to a daily practice of mental repetition for three hours. It was very difficult at first. I was restless. My body was undisciplined and would move around. My mind was constantly wandering. My legs hurt. I wanted to do everything else but mantras. My mind was resisting, but after time and constant practice, I began to enjoy my long practices doing my mantras. After completing my sadhana, I would be full of energy. I even remember those beautiful moments that I was able to be in deep meditation and connect with my soul, yet I could still hear my mind reciting the mantras over and over again. Such moments brought a lot of joy, love, and peace into my being. It requires discipline to sit for three hours. And even for you, especially in the beginning, it may take a little time to get used to sitting for five or ten minutes. What is most important is that you do the mantra no matter what. When you do it, you reap the positive results.

As I mentioned before, there are many mantras out there. In Hindu culture, they have so many mantras because they have so many wishes. Unfortunately, they have created a multitude of mantras and rituals with the hope that a *deva* (angel) will hear their mantra and grant them their wishes. Hindu mantras are not necessarily universal mantras. That goes the same for Buddhist mantras.

One thing about mantras is that it is a science. Mantras are not prayers. Mantras should also be recited without expectation. When there is expectation it means you are not reciting the mantras wholeheartedly. When there is expectation, meditation and spirituality are far away from you. How do you expect to burn karma at all when you are focused on expecting results? When you do anything selflessly, without expectation, that is when karma dissolves. It's absurd how far society has gone with mantras for everything. They have "Mantras for a Husband," "Mantras for a Wife," "Mantras to bear a Child." What is even crazier is that they even charge hundreds of dollars for it. In the 1970s, a popular guru by the name of Maharishi Mahesh Yogi charged money for mantras. He was the founder of Transcendental Meditation, whom many celebrities, including Oprah, follow today. If you want to be truly spiritual, don't get trapped.

A universal mantra that will help you on so many levels is the mantra: *Aum Namo Siddhaanam*. This is the first universal mantra ever created. It means "I bow to all siddhas." Siddhas are liberated souls. They do not have any karma, pain, and suffering. They are no longer in the cycle of birth and death. They reached enlightenment in their last human life and will not be born again. They are completely liberated. Their souls are fully expanded. They are merged with God. They are pure soul. They are free. Becoming a siddha is our true freedom.

By reciting this mantra, the way the Prakrit sounds are created, it means you not only bow to one siddha, you bow to all siddhas. The Prakrit word Siddhaanam reflects the plural form. Most mantras are singular, for example a popular one: "Aum Namah Shivaya," which translates to, "I bow to Shiva." It shows how limited it is. It is bowing to only one soul. Siddhaanam reflects all liberated souls.

Reciting Aum Namo Siddhaanam creates seeds of spirituality, activates your first chakra, brings you Godly light, creates red color around you, brings you right vision, right knowing, and right conduct.

You can recite this mantra at any time: right before your meals, while you are walking, driving, eating, as a spiritual practice, and even while sleeping. Yes, sleeping! It requires a lot of awareness though.

I travelled to India in 2012 and stayed at Acharya Shree's ashram in Delhi—Yogeesh Ashram International—for a week. One day I was resting and reciting mantras repeatedly in my mind. It was a nine-line mantra, which you will learn later. I was sleeping with awareness for three hours. I didn't realize how many mantra repetitions I did until I asked Acharya Shree. He said that I had repeated this nine-line mantra, while sleeping, over fifteen hundred times. Sometimes it can happen. My suggestion is to first learn how to recite mantras while awake for extended periods of time, then think about mantras while sleeping later.

It is important to begin developing a routine of spiritual practices. I highly suggest reciting mantras as part of your daily routine. The more energy you create, the more you will grow. You will always move forward when you put effort into your path.

Activity: Mantra recitation.

Recite *Aum Namo Siððhaanam* a minimum of one hundred and eight times. Pronounced (om na-mo sid-dhaa-nung). You can do this by sitting quietly in a chair or on the floor. Have your back straight. Touch your index finger and thumb together. And repeat out loud or in your mind. I would suggest out loud in the beginning, this way you can hear yourself pronounce the mantra correctly. After you complete at least one hundred and eight repetitions, close your eyes for one minute, relax, visualize red light, and enjoy the peace.

Mantras are divine and will help you return to your divinity. You will learn more about mantras in future chapters. It is a core spiritual practice, which should be understood and practiced deeply.

# :: BREATHING ::

Take a big deep breath right now.

I'm almost 100% certain that your shoulders and chest moved up right now. Most people are chest breathers. They breathe very shallowly. They were not born as chest breathers. Chest breathing was learned unconsciously over time. Look at a baby. They breathe from their belly. Why do they breathe from their belly? No stress. No tension. Peace. If you lie down with your back to the floor, you will notice that you automatically breathe with your belly.

Naturally you are a belly breather—that is when you inhale through your nose and your belly (diaphragm) expands and fills with air, and slowly deflates as you exhale. Like a balloon. It is very important to gain awareness how you breathe. It can help you in so many ways. If you are angry, upset, or nervous, your breath will calm you down. If you are tired and do some breathing exercises, you will gain physical energy. If you are going to sit for meditation, awareness of your breath will help you focus. If you are doing yoga, your breath will help you hold your pose. If you are a singer or speaker, you know that your talent relies on belly breathing for power, volume, and to save your vocal chords. If you are anxious or prone to panic attacks, the breath will save you. The key to putting breathwork into practice is having awareness. Awareness will help create the habit to breathe from your belly and not from your chest. The first thing you ever did as a baby when you entered this world was to take a deep breath. Breath is life. On average, you might take twelve to twenty breaths per minute as an adult. Your life will change when those twelve to twenty breaths come from your belly and not the chest.

The breath is powerful and it needs to be mastered. When you breathe from your diaphragm, it signifies you are balanced and connected to yourself. Chest breathers are those who live by the mind. Belly breathers are those who live by their soul. Live by your soul.

When I first met Acharya Shree I was somewhat aware about the importance of baby breathing (belly breathing). I had learned from yoga and meditation class to always take a deep breath and expand my belly. I knew about it, but I didn't practice it. Like anything else, once a master points out something that you are doing wrong or have a bad habit of, you know it needs to be corrected. One day Acharya Shree pointed out to me, "Your breath is too shallow. Take a deep breath in." I did and, of course, my chest and shoulders went up. "You need to work on breathing from your belly. You will feel a lot better. Your anxiety and nervousness will go away. Working on your breath is not to be taken lightly or disregarded. It's important. You need to focus on it so you can be balanced. You need to reconnect with yourself." In the early days, when meeting with Acharya Shree, I always sought big answers. I wanted all the steps to enlightenment, or even the entire science of karma, so my soul could be freed...and all in thirty days. I was eager, impatient, excited, and lacked understanding. Don't be like me. Before the big things, master the little things. How can I master myself and all of my lower qualities if I can't even master my breath?

Breathing. It's a simple thing. Right? Not so much. Especially when you've lived most of your life not breathing the right way. That's why you need to increase your awareness. The more you become aware of your breath, the more you

Sadhvi Siddhali Shree

automatically become physically, emotionally, and mentally better. When your mind and body are healthy and happy, the soul has a good instrument to work with in order to grow spiritually.

After Acharya Shree pointed out my lack of proper breathing, after time and with lots of practice of increasing awareness, I began to breathe from my belly. As of right now, 60% of the time I breathe from my belly naturally. I'm also working on increasing my awareness to breathe correctly even more. According to Acharya Shree, 50% is very good. Start focusing on your breath.

Breath work is very important and provides many benefits to you. First and foremost, it is your means to survive. Breath brings the oxygen supply to your body—vital organs, brain, nerves, glands. Proper breathing can help reduce or prevent diseases in the body. Spiritually speaking, when you have a strong, healthy, and oxygenated body and brain, you are more positive, have clarity, and have an awesome instrument to help you burn your karma. A weak body cannot burn as much karma as a strong body.

You want to be free? Master your breath.

Later, I will teach you different breathing techniques

which create a lot of heat and fire inside your body. These techniques will help you expel suppressed toxins in your body. These toxins create disease, negativity, and confusion. The fire from the breathing techniques also helps burn your karma. But before jumping ahead, you must learn deep breathing so that it becomes natural for you (again) and you do not have to think about it. Remember, you need a healthy body to practice spirituality. Breathwork is your first step to a healthy body.

Activity: Breathe.

Go outside and take seven deep breaths of fresh air.

When you take a deep breath, inhale through your nose, make sure your belly expands first, then hold your breath for seven seconds, then slowly exhale. After seven deep breaths, stretch out your arms to the sky, close your eyes, and look up towards the sky, then do another set of seven deep breaths. Afterwards, sit down wherever you are outside, close your eyes, and relax for one minute. Notice the difference of how you were feeling before taking deep breaths and after.

Daily Activity: Breathwork.

Throughout the day, do a breath check. See if you are breathing through your chest or with your belly. If you were breathing with your chest, switch back to breathing with your belly.

Deep breathing will help you become healthier and help make your mind clearer. Increase your awareness to breathe from your belly and not your chest throughout the day. The more you breathe from your belly, the more you will connect to yourself, live without stress, be more peaceful, and release tension. You deserve happy living. Deep breathing can free you.

# :: AWARENESS ::

Your spiritual growth is dependent on your ability to practice awareness. Awareness is your conscious ability to observe your thoughts, intentions, feelings, desires, habits, actions, and speech. With awareness, you will be able to transform your lower qualities into higher qualities, break negative habits and replace them with positive ones, notice areas in your life that need improvement, change your behavior to reflect spiritual living, observe when you are thinking negatively and immediately shift your thoughts towards positive thinking and much more. Awareness is like bringing a light to an undiscovered and untouched dark cave. The more light in the cave, the less likely you will fall, hurt yourself, or run into a wall, and the more you will discover what gems and treasures are hidden inside. Awareness is a skill that is developed with time and lots of practice. It needs to touch all aspects of your life, especially thoughts, actions, and speech since that is where most karma is collected.

It took me some time to understand what awareness really meant. When I first started my spiritual path, I began practicing awareness by noticing my thoughts. I didn't realize how negatively I used to think—about myself, others and the world. I actually considered myself a very positive person until I really began to observe the voice (thoughts) inside my head. I only associated awareness with observing thoughts. After meeting Acharya Shree, I gained a deeper understanding of awareness, and that it really touches all aspects of life.

During his talks with me about my anger he would say, "You need to work on your anger. You are too angry. Your mind is too violent. Practice awareness." With my rebellious, sarcastic, and immature self I would reply, "Well yes, Acharya Shree, I am aware that I get angry. That's why I need your help. I want you to fix my anger. I'm aware I have anger." Being aware that you have lower qualities is the first step to self-improvement. If you are unaware, you cannot improve it. Over time, I realized what he meant.

Awareness is like shining a light on a demonic-monster

that hates the light. The more light that is shined upon it, the less power it has. With persistent *light-shining*, awareness, we gain our power back and the demonic-monster no longer has control over our lives. We are no longer slaves to our inner enemies. We are free from those chains.

When we choose to practice awareness, we voluntarily engage in an inner battle with all of our inner enemies. And there are many enemies. Sometimes all surface at the same time. Sometimes maybe a few lower qualities are on the surface.

For example, as a spiritual person wishing to remove all the darkness and ignorance that covers your soul, you will one day have to face your anger. Even if you think you are not an angry person, it may not be on the surface right now, but anger is hidden in you. All it takes is one random person to push one of your buttons, and it's there—thriving and alive. When your anger, aka one of the demonic-monsters, is on the surface, by making your face turn red, your heart pump faster, your face frown, or allowing bad words to come out of your mouth, your anger-monster is used to taking over and sending you a bunch of thoughts that are often irrelevant, make you overthink, and hardly ever provide any solution. But because you are a spiritual person who is dedicated to improving yourself, you are voluntarily choosing to enter battle by practicing awareness. When you shine your light of awareness on your anger-monster you might start thinking differently: "Why am I angry? This serves no purpose. Anger is useless. It's hurting me more than anyone else. The real me has no anger. Where are my love, compassion, and understanding in this moment? I should forgive, not hate. I should listen, not be stubborn. Do I really need to be right, right now?" In the beginning of practicing awareness, the anger-monster will resist you even more and become stubborn. It wants you to be angry. It wants to be in control of you. As a spiritual person, you want your soul to be in control. Awareness helps you do just that. Your anger (anger-monster) will not disappear overnight, but with consistent practice and awareness, it will be less and less.

When I first met Acharya Shree, I was a very angry person. I didn't realize it because I was so used to suppressing my anger and "forgiving" people. I don't think I ever really forgave, I think I pretended nothing ever happened and pushed my anger behind a door, closed it, never opened it… and smiled. I didn't realize that by not expressing my anger, I was hurting myself more. Anger kills us before anyone else. I thought suppression and controlling my anger was what a *spiritual person* did. I didn't realize I'd have to face everything I stowed away. As a master, Acharya Shree's job is to press all my buttons so that all my demonic-monsters can come out.

When I first became a monk and when my training really began, Acharya Shree was pushing all my buttons, left and right, relentlessly. Never a moment to breathe. I would get upset, thinking he had no compassion for me. In reality, he has the most compassion. He is freeing me from chains that I had no idea had a strong grip on me. When I first moved to the ashram, I would hold in my anger for days, sometimes weeks, at a time. Now, if you ask Acharya Shree, anger is one of my greatest improvements, and when I do get angry, it is only for a moment. I credit having the guidance of an enlightened master for that and my own practice of self-awareness.

Anger is one example of an area in our lives that needs constant awareness. Everyone has it. Including you. And we all need to work on it. Anger can sneak up out of the blue and make us upset the entire day, if we let it. As awareness increases within us, anger's (or any other negativity we have) affect and power on us will be less and less. With awareness, the soul gains back its control.

Awareness not only helps us battle the enemies we have inside now, but it helps us avoid collecting any more bad karma. And of course we need to stop collecting more pollution around our souls. As you grow spiritually and begin to understand deeper concepts and higher principles to live by, you will begin to look at life with different eyes. For example, you have already been introduced to nonviolence. When you practice awareness regarding nonviolence, you will see the world with new eyes. You will begin to become aware of your violent thoughts, your violent actions, and your violent speech. As your awareness about nonviolence increases, maybe you will think more positively, you might not step on the spider to kill it but rather take it outside and save its life, and instead of using harsh language out of anger, you might hold your tongue and be wise enough to say the right words as to not hurt someone else's feelings. Because of the awareness, we automatically begin shifting our thoughts, actions, and speech. As we shift into awareness, we collect less karma or stop collecting karma entirely. Less karma. Less chains. Less suffering.

The challenges in this book will require awareness on your part. Awareness will develop slowly. You need to make awareness your greatest strength and skill. You need it for your spiritual path to battle all the negativities that will surface as part of your journey. Awareness is your greatest friend. It is the light that helps remove the darkness from your soul.

Acharya Shree once told me, "Awareness automatically reduces the power of anything negative that exists in you. If by chance you forget to practice awareness, it's okay. Try to remember next time. Awareness is the number one key to free you. Everything else is second. Increase your awareness on a daily basis. Awareness leads to understanding. Understanding burns your illusions. Awareness and understanding lead you to right vision."

Activity: Reflect and write.

What are some things that you are aware of that you need to work on and improve? How do you think you can implement practicing awareness on a daily basis?

Awareness is light to free your soul from the darkness. Practice it. Increase it. Use it. Awareness will free you from all of your inner chains, enemies, and monsters.

# :: TRATKA ::

Awareness must be developed in order to awaken your soul. Alongside awareness, you must also learn how to concentrate. Concentration is your ability to focus your mind on a single point. The more concentration power you have the deeper you can go into your soul.

The power of concentration is like holding a magnifying glass to the floor and allowing the sunlight to shine through. If the sunlight is focused by the magnifying glass enough, you can burn yourself or a piece of paper. The reason this happens is because all of the surrounding particles are brought into one focal point, one stream, of light. When the particles are not scattered, there is power in them. The same concept applies to your mind. If your thoughts are scattered and all over the place, it will be difficult to focus in meditation, and of course in daily life, such as in school, work, business, and creation. Focus and concentration are needed in order to progress and advance.

Most people give up on meditation because they lack the ability to focus and concentrate. Too many thoughts attack them during those moments that they want the inner quiet, peace, and solitude. Like anything else, it takes practice to develop a skill. As your concentration and focus power improves, you will be able to go deeper and deeper into your consciousness.

There are so many clouds that cover the soul. The clouds are in forms of thoughts, karma, and much more, which block your soul's light. The stronger your concentration power, the more you can pierce through the clouds, the pollution, and begin to taste bliss.

In my early years of meditation, I would sit for thirty to forty-five minutes. Most of the time I was trying to bypass my mind and not pay attention to any thoughts. I was doing my best to concentrate and not get distracted. Once I got to a point in my meditation, my body and mind would relax and let go for a moment, maybe three to five seconds, and I would taste my soul for the brief encounter. Forty-five minutes is worth sitting for a five second taste of soul. Acharya Shree says those five seconds are the real meditation, because you're with your self, your soul.

Concentration power helps you enter meditation and sustain your meditation. Start small. It's not easy to stay in deep meditation because the mind and thoughts love to sneak in and disturb you, and your body constantly reminds you how uncomfortable it is. When you have concentration power, you increase your skill to ignore your body, mind, or any outer distractions. You are fully in tune and immersed in yourself. It's the greatest feeling to be truly one with yourself and I can't wait for you to experience it.

I remember I would ask Acharya Shree how I could be like other meditators and sit for three hours, eight hours or even ten hours in meditation. I used to want to be like others. Acharya Shree would laugh and say, "They are not even in meditation. They are in their minds. They are in imagination. Soul has nothing to do with that. They would be lucky to get a glimpse even for ten seconds out of their eight hour practice. People have the wrong idea. It's not how long someone can meditate that defines a good meditator. What matters is the quality of the meditation. If you are able to taste soul for five to ten seconds you are very lucky. It's very rare for practitioners to even experience two minutes of deep meditation and total connection with soul. Don't compare yourself. Meditate. Relax. Let go. Increase your soul-time, not your mind-time."

Meditation is like entering the dark, infinite sky. There is so much to discover, see, and realize about your soul. It's endless. Concentration power is your fuel to propel yourself into the unknown. As you continue to grow more and more, the unknown will be known. This is self-realization. It's possible. What you are seeking is possible. Knowing yourself is possible. Tasting the depths of your beautiful and amazing soul is possible. Patience and persistence will get you there. Concentration is a must in order to know yourself.

Today, I'd like to share with you a meditation technique that will help you increase your concentration and focus power. It will feel uncomfortable at first, but keep at it. It is called Tratka.

Tratka is a practice where you stare at a black quarter size dot on a piece of white paper without blinking your eyes. This practice helps you release all your tension and stress. According to Acharya Shree, most stress is collected through eyesight as a result of disliking something. That's why when you are stressed-out, you might touch your eyes or the top of the bridge of your nose. Later, your neck and shoulders become very tense and full of knots because they are the closest muscles to your eyes, where the tension can stay. The stress held in your neck, shoulders, and eyes can be released, and this can bring you a lot of relief. The way this stress is collected is the same way it must be released—through the eyes. As you begin to stare at the black dot without blinking your eyes, you will begin to feel a slight burning sensation. This is normal. It shows the technique is working. After some time, the burning sensation will fade and your eyes will begin to tear. The tears are releasing the stress. Let the tears fall by themselves. As much as you would like to, still do not blink. Once you blink the practice is over. The goal is to concentrate on the black dot with open eyes and without blinking. With time and practice your concentration power increases, and more and more stress will leave you. Like any technique, it takes time to get better at it. In the beginning, you might be able to do this technique for thirty seconds or one minute, but after six months of daily practice you might be able to do it for –thirty to forty-five minutes. Two of Acharya Shree's current monks-in-training, Miles & Anubhuti, both learned the technique and are able to practice tratka up to fifty minutes while standing on one foot. They both learned this technique during the Meditation Retreat Workshop at Siddhayatan and, after much practice, they have become experts at the technique.

You are getting daily tools and advice to help you progress on the path. They are guaranteed to work if you practice them and put them to use. If you do not use your tools, you cannot build a house. Use your spiritual tools and set your soul free.

Activity: Practice Tratka.

Get a piece of blank printer paper. With a black marker, color in a black quarter size dot in the center of the paper. Tape the piece of paper to a wall. Sit eighteen to twenty-four inches away from the wall, with the dot at eye level. Make sure there is no fan or air conditioning on in the room, as the air flow can hurt your eyes. Then proceed to stare at the black dot without blinking your eyes. Try this practice a few times and extend your time as long as you can tolerate. Anyone can practice this technique, except if you have glaucoma.

It is very important to develop your concentration and focus power in order to help you grow spiritually. Concentration in combination with awareness will help you transform immensely and dive deeply into the endless infinite ocean of your soul.

# :: NON-ATTACHMENT ::

The two roots that keep us in the cycle of birth and death, the cycle of pain and pleasure, and far away from liberation are attachment and hatred—like and dislike. If it wasn't for our like and dislike, attachment (raga) and hatred (dvesha), our souls would be free. Like and dislike are the glue that attach the karmic particles to the soul. Like and dislike are the main sources of our illusion, ignorance, and stress. Where does like and dislike come from? It comes from our fascination and motivation to fulfill our desires.

If we like something, we want our desires fulfilled. If we dislike something, we do not want that particular desire fulfilled. If we are beyond liking or disliking anything, it shows we are non-attached. Since our five senses and mind are so strong, they create the strong desire, motivation, and inspiration to fulfill them. Desires belong to sense-pleasure and sense-fulfillment. And the mind can go very far to convince us how bad we need something, even though we really don't.

The five avenues to like/dislike something are through our five senses. We can enjoy a touch or feel uncomfortable by a touch. We may not like hot or cold water, but we do like warm water. We can really enjoy a particular smell or be turned off by it. We may like the smell of roses but do not like the smell of jasmine. We might like looking at one thing, but not really be interested in looking at something else. We might like looking at sculptures, but dislike looking at pictures from war. We might like eating particular foods because they taste so good and sweet, but we may also dislike particular vegetables because they are bitter. And lastly, we might enjoy only sweet words or classical music with a distaste for abusive language and disco music. Everything we think and do is based on if we like something or dislike something through our senses. Our five senses pass on information to our brains and the mind decides and interprets if it likes or dislikes something. Disliking can cause us stress, disappointment, revenge, and dissatisfaction. Liking can bring us temporary happiness. The way society works—businesses, entertainment, and marketing companies—is that they try to discover all your unfulfilled desires and then create solutions to help you fulfill them. Or, it may create a perfect ideal life in your mind, that if you have certain things in life, you will be happy. That is the role of society. To keep you in society. Society will create desires/problems in your life and society will play the role of solving them. (Oh society, you are my hero. You have all the solutions. Please take all my money too. I will be very happy.) C'mon really? Soul does not belong to the society. The role of spirituality, is to take you out of it—to free your soul.

How do you accomplish this? Get rid of your desires. Get rid of your likes and dislikes. Practice non-attachment. Be neutral. Be balanced.

Soul is desireless.

Okay, one exception. It desires liberation.

Your desires and attachments keep you bound to this world. As the enlightened Tirthankara Mahavir said, "Your desires are limitless like the sky." If desires are as limitless as the sky, then the path to freedom is not that way. We need to put an end to our desires. Or if there is no end to all of your desires, at least take a new approach. Instead of desiring a new car, a new look, a better body, or money in the bank account, desire that your anger disappear from you, desire that your ego be crushed so you can become a more humble person, or desire that lust be removed from your mind. Fulfill those *spiritual desires* by taking action and working on yourself.

The popular best-selling book and movie, *The Secret*, encourages you to "manifest your desires and dreams." The irony in *The Secret* is that it keeps you bound to the world of pseudo-happiness, pain and suffering. The real secret is to have no desires. When you have no desires, you are free. You have no chains bound to your soul. If you like or don't like something, it doesn't matter. It doesn't bother you. It doesn't affect you. That's freedom.

Why are we afraid of what people think? Because we are afraid they will dislike us, and deep down all we want is to be liked. If you let go of the need to be liked or disliked, you will say whatever you want to say without any fear. You will have freedom of expression. You will feel that you can be who you really are. If there are no likes or dislikes, there is no fear. The same applies to people. If you like someone, and they do something you dislike, you may end up not being their friend. If you really dislike someone, you will then be angry and may even become hateful. If you like someone, you might love them. Both like and dislike, love and hate, make you suffer. Both like and dislike bring you karma.

I know. I know. That karma word. Karma is a blinder. Karma brings clouds to your soul. It's interesting. When you meet a person for the first time and by chance *fall in love* you become blind. You can't think or see clearly. You are taken by that blindness. Love is blind. The same rule applies to karma. You like something so much, you collect karma, it blinds your soul. You dislike something so much, you collect karma, it blinds your soul. Soul is stuck yet again.

Like and dislike make you suffer. That's a pretty bold statement. When you love, you suffer. When you hate, you suffer. So don't love or hate. Just be. Be one with all living beings. It shows you are separate from them. According to society's definition of love, it seems to be more of a verb. Love is a noun. A oneness. When you are in oneness with anything, there is no room for like or dislike. Like and dislike belong to duality. Soul is only one reality.

Non-Attachment, like and dislike, attachment and hatred is a huge subject. In essence, your attachments make you suffer, whether they are positive or negative attachments. If you like something and it is gone, you suffer. That is why the death of a loved one is so painful. We are hurting because of our own attachment to that person.

It is important to bring up attachment and how to practice

non-attachment, because practicing spirituality without the understanding of non-attachment will keep you bound to this world.

I want you to know from the beginning of your spiritual journey (or wherever you are at now), that you will need to work on your attachments and desires. If not now (and that is okay), at some point in your path you will.

The spiritual path and your practices are meant to reduce the power of your senses and their control over you and giving back power to your soul. As you work on understanding the soul, go beyond like and dislike, and reduce the power of the senses. Then you will continue on the path towards your soul's freedom.

Activity: Reflect and write.

In your journal, identify your desires. Who are you attached to? Why are you attached to them? What are you attached to? How can these likes/dislikes hold you back?

Non-attachment will free your soul. When you are not living in one extreme of like or dislike, you are living a life of true spiritual balance. When balanced, those three gems: right knowledge, right vision, and right action, are near.

# :: MEDITATION ::

There are many reasons why you should meditate. It helps you physically, emotionally, mentally, and spiritually in so many ways. These days meditation is becoming quite popular, even though it has been practiced for centuries. Despite its proven history, the many benefits, and how it will lead to your soul's awakening, enlightenment, and ultimately your liberation, when it is time to sit on the floor and actually meditate, it's extremely difficult.

Meditation has no *quick-fix*. You cannot one day just decide to meditate and enter the deepest states of consciousness. If it were that easy, everyone would be extremely peaceful, balanced, calm, compassionate, and understanding these days, especially with how popular it is. Meditation is one of those things in life towards which you have to put a lot of effort; it requires commitment, daily motivation, inspiration, and patience.

I understand those moments when you hear great things about meditation and you are excited at the possibility of connecting to your soul and then when you sit down, close your eyes, and take a deep breath, all you can do is think. Think. Think. The mind doesn't want you to improve yourself. It doesn't want the soul to be in control. That is why as soon as you sit down, your mind will attack you. The mind is such a great obstacle, however, the more you grow in practicing awareness, increasing your concentration power, doing your breathing techniques, mantras, etc., meditation will happen. One thing is sure: you cannot give up on meditation. That's like giving up on yourself and I know you are not about that.

In order to grow spiritually and know your soul, the mind needs to have less power over you. Most *spiritual teachings* today focus on ego. They have gotten stuck on ego. The reality is, the ego is only one type of blockage. Did you know the food you eat also affects your mind, thus affecting your ability to meditate? Did you know that if your five senses are too much into desires, it blocks meditation? Your stress, tension, and built-up toxins also block your meditation. These things affect your mind, give strength to your mind, so it's no wonder that meditation can be difficult to enter. It doesn't mean that meditation is impossible. It means not only do you need to work on closing your eyes, relaxing, and learning to concentrate, but you also need to work on all aspects of your life. That is what spirituality is about. It's not just yoga or meditation or being ego-less. Spirituality is a total change in lifestyle based on the awareness and effort that you want to awaken and liberate your soul.

So what does this mean? It means you should consider eating lighter foods. Become vegetarian. How do you expect to meditate, which requires a lot of energy, when most of your energy is being used by your digestive system to break down all the heavy meat (beef, pork, chicken, and fish)? Want to enter deep states? You need let go of the foods that weigh you down, take up your energy, and of course eliminate foods that cause violence and pain. How can you enter a state of divinity, when you just ate a hamburger, which could have been made up of a mix of meat from one hundred cows? Spirituality is something you don't pick and choose. If you want to be spiritual, follow the path fully.

Work on reducing the power of your senses. The food, your senses, and thoughts feed the mind. Lighter foods, non-attachment to your senses' desires, and lighter thoughts will allow you to meditate. You need to purify your body and mind.

So many things chain your soul down. In reality, it's all karma that blocks the soul, but the things you think about, the things you do, the things you say, the things you eat, the things you want are all weights. Meditation happens when you are light, when you are relaxed. That's why you feel like you are floating and might feel that you are even out of the body. Meditation happens when you are light, not heavy.

Here's something to think about: If someone is in the river and does not know how to swim, they will resist, they will kick, they will scream, and ultimately they will get tired and drown if they don't get help. Why? Because they created so much tension, stress, and fatigue because of resistance and fear. However, if the person instead became relaxed, accepted the situation, and didn't resist it, they would float along the river's surface. In the same way, the mind is resisting and trying to stop you from entering meditation. Instead of giving up or getting frustrated, accept that the mind is being anxious or upset for a moment, but commit to learning how to relax in the moment. When you relax, meditation automatically begins. With time, the mind will be your soul's servant, not master. Right now, you are a slave to your mind. That's why you are reading this book—to change that.

Most people do not know how to relax, that is why I am sharing with you different techniques and advice to help you relax and make your body and mind purer and lighter. I've had my share of frustrating moments: meditations with no experiences, a feeling I was wasting my time with no results, but I'm glad I kept at it and now experience what real meditation is about—soul.

Deep breathing will help you relax, tratka will help you focus, awareness will help you become less affected by your thoughts, eating light foods helps to save energy (and not collect more karma pollution), and mantras will give your mind something to do as your soul enters into meditation.

Activity: Twenty minutes meditation.

Set aside time today to totally relax for twenty minutes. In your bedroom, set up a candle and put on peaceful music if you would like to help switch your mood. Sit comfortably for a few minutes and practice deep breathing. After a few minutes, lie down comfortably on the floor, close your eyes, and relax. Let go of your body. Let go of your mind. Enjoy the moments of stillness and peace.

Meditation is your ticket to freedom. Master yourself. Master meditation. Then you will meet your Inner Master.

# :: LIKE YOURSELF ::

When you have yourself, you have everything.

Life will always be incomplete or unfulfilling unless you have yourself. You can be in the greatest relationship of your life, being in love with another person, yet despite this relationship, still feel you are lacking love. Or maybe you have accomplished many great things in life. Perhaps you are considered by your family and friends as a successful person, yet you think you have not achieved anything. Or maybe all of your coworkers believe you to be a very confident individual that speaks his or her mind without hesitation, yet you consider yourself inferior, shy, and possibly not good enough. The world will view you one way, that is sure. But what is important is how you view yourself. You live with yourself every day, in each and every moment. No one else does. No one hears or sees what is going inside you on a daily basis. Do you like yourself? Do your love yourself?

Everyone wants to be happy. You want to be happy. I want to be happy. One of the first steps to happiness is learning to like yourself. You need to like yourself and love yourself for who you are. When you like yourself 100%, the stress and pain will disappear from your life.

We have been taught by society to not like ourselves. Society has created this idea of perfection, and no one has ever been the icon or symbol of perfection. Perfection does not exist. There is no perfect person. No perfect path. No perfect anything. Yet we compare ourselves to this nonexistent idea of perfection. The need to be perfect creates the internal voices of self-hate, self-judgment, and self-dislike in us: we can never be good enough, we will never be successful, we will never be deserving; we will never matter, and we will always be worthless. These are scary thoughts if you believe them.

Society says you need to have perfect skin, perfect hair, perfect body-shape, a perfect job, be wealthy, be highly educated and be perfectly smart with no room for error. No crinkles in your pants, no spills of coffee on your shirt, no hair out of its place, no hair on your body, perfectly sized and perky breasts, perfect penis size, perfect butt, perfect legs, perfect grades, perfect face (no pimples, acnes, blemishes, or hairy moles allowed), perfect nails, perfect skin tone, and perfect feet. Oh yeah, not to mention, perfect family, perfect house, perfect looking husband or wife, perfect looking kids who are perfectly smart, perfect health, and perfect social status, perfect reputation, perfect spirituality. You need to be absolutely perfect.

What a list. Have you started laughing yet?

Geezus, no wonder we are all stressed out.

It's absurd.

In this perfect ideal world that we try so hard to live by and never meet the expectations of, there is no room for error because, by golly, you are going to be JUDGED by the ruthless flames of society. You are going to be judged by society and people all around you. You are going to be judged. But you know what the sad thing is about this list of perfection, is that *you* are the biggest judge of yourself.

You dislike yourself—if not entirely, some parts.

It's time to change that around. Like yourself. Like all aspects of you. You're an amazing person, I'm sure.

If we let go of the need to be perfect, our lives will totally change. If we like and love ourselves as we are, stress will leave our lives. The energy that goes into fearing rejection or worrying about what others think of us will disappear and we will have so much energy freed up that we can use for spiritual practices.

Say good-bye to society. Society tells you to dislike yourself. Listen to your soul instead. Like and love yourself. There is true freedom in that.

Want to be happy?

You are the answer.

One thing is sure: it's okay to improve ourselves. Especially for the spiritual path, we need to improve ourselves and become wiser, better, and more compassionate people. Being driven towards self-improvement and to grow spiritually is a choice we make for ourselves because WE want to be better, not to be better for others. And definitely not to prove something to society.

When you have yourself, you have everything. It means you like and love yourself. You are complete within yourself. You do not rely on anyone else's or society's approval and validation. You have so much love towards yourself, that if by chance you are alone, you are not lonely—you have unconditional self-love. When you give meaning to your own life by deciding what your purpose is and living for yourself and no one else, you will be fulfilled and live a meaningful life. When you believe in yourself, you are totally confident. When you are satisfied with life and what you have, there is no discontentment or stress. When you are proud of yourself and your own accomplishments, you do not rely on someone praising or appreciating you. When you are balanced, you are not affected if someone says anything negative. When you are spiritual, you are in tune with soul.

Say good-bye to perfection and disliking yourself. Like and love yourself. Appreciate yourself. Be proud of yourself. Inspire yourself. Awaken yourself. Embrace the freedom.

Activity: Love yourself.

Take a moment to look in the mirror and say "I like myself." "I love myself." And look at yourself for at least three minutes trying to feel that like and love towards yourself.

In your journal, list the things you like and dislike about yourself. How has the idea of perfection kept you away from being happy with yourself? How will your life change if you started liking and loving yourself?

Make liking and loving yourself a daily practice.

# :: MANTRAS ::

Mantras, divine sounds, will give you different results based on the combination given. One mantra may help you create energy to increase your concentration and learning ability, whereas another mantra will create protective energy around you so that you do not get affected too much by negative people or a negative situation. There are many mantras out there that can be used for different things. As I mentioned before, I am going to share with you universal mantras. They do not belong to any particular religion, they can be used by anyone, and they are for spiritual growth.

The first two mantras I learned from the Hindu group I initially belonged to (before meeting Acharya Shree), were the

Gayatri and Mahamrityunjaya mantras. Because I was not familiar with mantras and didn't know that there were many, I assumed these were the only two mantras to recite and that they were the *only way* towards spiritual growth. I was extremely attached to these mantras because they were the first to bring me some peace. I rejected anything else.

When I attended my first satsang (spiritual gathering) at Acharya Shree's ashram, Yogeesh Ashram, in Riverside, California, and was handed a mantra paper, I immediately felt resistance. I wasn't open to learning new mantras. I strongly believed the two I had learned already were all that I'd ever need. Also, I believed I knew more about *real spirituality* than those who were sitting in the room. I had a really big ego about my spiritual knowledge in those days. Only later did I finally realize and accept that I didn't know anything at all. Acharya Shree always says, "What you think you know, you don't. What you don't know, you do." During that first mantra session with the group, I didn't sing along until the Gayatri and Mahamrityunjaya mantras came up. I laugh now at how resistant I was.

When something that is good for you is given to you, you resist it and turn your head away. Like a baby who does not want to. "It's good for you," you say. But the baby still turns her head. An enlightened master was sharing with me universal mantras that would help me grow, but I had no clue. I resisted the goodness. I resisted soul food.

The reason I resisted the universal mantras so much was because I was afraid I was worshipping something or someone I didn't know. I didn't believe in worship. After being a Catholic for so long, I didn't want to end up a follower of anything or be part of any organized religion. The unfamiliar mantras scared me. In truth, I feared repeating mantras that I didn't know about or understand that they were good for me. I was resistant because I feared it.

If you are experiencing similar feelings as I bring up mantras or other aspects of spirituality, I understand. You know that you are searching for truth and you don't want to hand over your trust and path to just anyone. By sharing my experiences, I hope you can relate and see that I truly want to help you grow and awaken and also not fall into the traps that I did.

After I received more guidance from Acharya Shree, I learned the meaning behind the mantras, and that I wasn't worshipping some random god or person. I learned it was a science of creating spiritual and positive energy around me; I opened up, my walls came down, and I was less resistant. I was again excited to learn about mantras. Deep down all I wanted was to grow. I was just scared of something unfamiliar and didn't want to fall into any traps. I was determined to protect my spirituality. The mantras mentioned in this book will help you. I appreciate your openness. The more you recite mantras in your life, the more you will begin to see the positive results.

I suggest to always do your mantras wholeheartedly, without expectation. Reciting mantras with a pure heart works better than with expectations for something in return. Create the energy and then let the energy work for you.

The more you *lose yourself* (like how time flies when you are enjoying a good time with a friend) in mantras and become in tune with them, the more chances you have in jumping right into meditation. When you are in meditation is when the karma and the pollution that surrounds your soul begin to burn. Use these mantras to your advantage. What you will learn today and in future days are powerful mantras that can transform your life. Most of my spiritual practices in my early years as a monk included reciting mantras. Acharya Shree reminded me often that I needed to create more and more spiritual energy around me if I wanted to grow higher and higher. Without energy, you cannot move forward. Without burning karma, the soul remains in the dark.

Today, I would like to share with you one of my favorite

mantras: *Aum Hrim Shrim Klim Arhum Hamsah*. It is pronounced like om hreeng shreeng kleeng ara-hung hung-suh. You can listen to the correct pronunciation at http://shinethroughwisdom.com/mantras.

This is a powerful mantra which helps detoxify you of poison and negativities. This applies to physical poison, disease, toxins, and mental and emotional negativities. Aum means God. Hrim represents extraordinary enlightened masters around the universe. *Shrim* is the sound for spiritual prosperity. *Klim* is the sound which removes poison and negativity, *Arhum* is the sound for all liberated souls (which is who you are striving to be), and *Hamsa* means swan. So by reciting this mantra, you remove negativities and purify yourself.

The main word in this mantra is Klim. You should recite klim hundreds to thousands of times if you are ever full of anger. Another tip for when you are angry is to drink a glass of cold water—it helps reduce your blood pressure. One thing to never do is go to sleep angry. You can collect bad karma in your sleep if you are violent. Any time you go to sleep, always fall asleep with peace in your heart. Recite klim anytime you are negative or angry, this way you come out of it. Don't expect your anger to just disappear after reciting it three times. You will need to recite it thousands of times. All things on the spiritual path require effort.

Klim can also be used to help someone heal.

My favorite aunt was diagnosed with colon cancer. By the time I was able to visit and try to help, it was already in the later stages. Death was inevitable. Regardless, I wanted to do something for her—for her soul—this way she would get some spiritual seeds for a future life. I also wanted to help reduce the pain she was experiencing. Fortunately, one night she was open to the family doing mantras and breathing techniques. One of the mantras we recited as a family was Aum Hrim Shrim Klim Arhum Hamsa. I focused the energy created from my family to go towards her. It was interesting to see my relatives doing the mantras because they were very Catholic, and doing mantras is far from their norm. Fortunately, they were open to it because they had hope for positive results. After the family and I did the mantras, I asked for some private time with her. I then recited "Aum Klim" over and over, as I placed my hands over her body, moving up and down from the feet to her head. I immediately felt the healing energy come from my hands. Acharya Shree had given me this mantra to recite over her. I did this practice for approximately twenty minutes. After I was done, my cousin came in and noticed that my aunt's face had reddened, showing there was increase of circulation and heat (energy) in her body. Though she passed away, before she died I encouraged her to meet Acharya Shree (for spiritual seeds). The doctors were surprised that she continued to live despite her state of health. Acharya Shree mentioned that the mantras I did for her and the fact she met him extended her life by three weeks.

Activity: Mantra recitation.

Recite *Aum Hrim Shrim Klim Arhum Hamsa* one hundred and eight times. Pronounced om hreeng shreeng kleeng arahung hung-suh. You can do this by sitting quietly on a chair or on the floor. Have your back straight. Place your hands on your knees, palms facing up. Repeat the mantra out loud or in your mind. After you complete at least one hundred and eight repetitions, close your eyes for one minute, relax, visualize white light, and enjoy the healing.

Mantras are beneficial for anyone — physically, emotionally, mentally, and spiritually. There is a power in mantras when you do them. Not only does it change you, but it begins to affect the people around you and where you live. Do your mantras always. Be open to it. It works. Practice.

# :: KAPALBHATI ::

Breath is your survival. Breath can also be your karma burner. Proper intensive breathing creates a fire-like heat in the body, which burns the toxins in your body. Toxins are the root cause of stress, anxiety, nervousness, disease, and much more. Toxins are essentially the physical manifestation of karma. Therefore it is very important to burn and expel your toxins, thus purifying your body. According to Acharya Shree the "sins" are "toxins." Both are impurities that block the soul.

Your body is karma. As a result of karma you have the particular body that you have. You were born to certain parents because of your karma. Based on the genetics that you inherited, those toxins in your blood need to be purified. When your body is purified, soul can grow and expand itself.

I used to think I was angry, stubborn, and hard-headed because it was part of my personality. Later I learned from Acharya Shree that these negative qualities were inherited. My soul is pure and divine, but my body was not. My lower qualities were embedded in my parents' blood, which then was passed on to me. I also grew up observing these lower qualities from my parents, and it became a part of my ideology and the way of living. I was born with it.

Why do we suffer and have pain? Because of the toxins in our blood. Unless we purify such toxins and karma manifested in the body, the soul cannot grow. In the Meditation Retreat I always mention, "You cannot get to soul unless you first purify your body, and then mind. Once you purify those two things, soul is right there."

We get the body we currently have as a result of our karma collected from previous lives—a combination of both good and bad karma. If we are lucky, all of our five senses work. But some of us don't have that. For example, some people are born deaf, blind, or mute. Some are born without the sense of smell. This is a result of karma. Maybe at some point they poked someone's eyes out, or sliced someone's ear off. I know it sounds wrong to say it, but there are reasons, as a result of karma, why the body does not appear normal or it does not function well. Maybe limbs are missing or look abnormal, maybe there is a chemical imbalance, maybe there is something wrong with the brain. Everything goes back to karma. What is great and awesome about the spiritual path is that you can do something about it. You can make an effort to change your body, change your mind, and change your life.

In order to achieve liberation you first need a pure body. As you work on purifying your body, you automatically begin strengthening it. A strong body is required to do spiritual practices. If you have a weak body it is difficult to do the practices that help you burn off your karma. For example, the breathing technique you will learn today can be very intensive. One professional boxer attended the Purnam Yoga Retreat at Siddhayatan. This boxer was an undefeated champion. When he started to learn the intensive breathing techniques, he was so shocked that it was a workout for his body. He trained so hard as a professional boxer, so he didn't think a yogic breathing technique would be so intensive. I'm not saying that you need to have a strong body like a professional boxer to start practicing intensive breathing exercises, however, you do need a strong and pure body to start burning off all that karma. You need to be strong on the spiritual path. You need to be a warrior...strong in your body and mind to battle your inner enemies. One day, you will conquer yourself.

A breathing technique that you need to start practicing is *kapalbhati*. Kapalbhati is popularly known as the "breath of fire." Kapalbhati means "purification of the skull." Through this intensive breathing technique, you bring in a lot of oxygen into your bloodstream. The oxygen, in combination with the heat created from the practice, begins to purify your blood, then purified blood goes to the brain. This technique will require constant practice. You have a lot of toxins to clear out of yourself.

For example, if you are a heavy meat eater, it will take six to seven years to purify your blood of all the animal toxins you brought into your body. And that is as a vegetarian. You can do the breathing technique as a meat eater, but it defeats the purpose. You are trying to close off all the open sources of karma. Being vegetarian and doing the purification breathing technique makes more sense, otherwise you continue to stay in the cycle. Cleaning your blood of animal toxins takes six to seven years and that is only one aspect of purification. You also have the karma and toxins you were born with—like anger, stubbornness, impatience, frustration, violent thoughts, insecurities, negativities, depression, and much more. There is so much to purify and that is why it takes time to work on yourself. As you purify yourself through kapalbhati, you will start to remove the karma pollution and begin to have clarity and spiritual understanding. Once you have clarity, the gem of right vision, happiness is with you.

Kapalbhati has many benefits. Most important, it burns and expels toxins from your body. It reduces high blood pressure. It can help heal early stage cancer. It increases focus and concentration. It helps eliminate confusion. It can stop negative thinking. It also burns fat. It's one of the best meditation breathing techniques. Kapalbhati burns your thoughts, which are also toxins. So when you sit to enter meditation after practicing kapalbhati, you will notice a difference in your practice.

Kapalbhati is one of the main breathing techniques for body-purification. If you do not learn any other breathing technique for the rest of your life, and you practice kapalbhati a lot, you will still reap many benefits. You do not need to be a yogic breathing master to advance on the spiritual path. You do, however, need a pure body and *pure skull*.

Activity: Breathe intensely.

Practice Kapalbhati at least one hundred times today. Watch Acharya Shree's video for an additional overview and demonstration:

https://www.youtube.com/watch?v=d6d7_oJGzKQ

Every day, for the next seven days, try to increase your kapalbhati practice by one hundred. This way by the seventh day, you are doing this breathing technique up to seven hundred times. Do not go over seven hundred times per day. You will notice a difference in the way you feel.

Breathing techniques are a must for the spiritual path, because they help create a strong and pure body. Breathing techniques also burn your toxins, which is karma. With practice, you will see positive results. If you only read about the breathing technique, don't expect any major life changes. Want results? Practice. Want spiritual growth? Practice.

Your path is always in your hands.

# :: MINIMIZE VIOLENCE ::

Nonviolence is the core of the spiritual path. Without integrating nonviolence into your life, understanding it, practicing it, and living with awareness about it, you will be far away from attaining your goals. My intention is not to discourage you, but to share with you the deeper teachings so you can practice spirituality to your full potential. You can practice yoga, meditation, mantras, and other techniques and it will be helpful. However, without nonviolence, higher levels of spirituality are not possible. Living a nonviolent life means to stop collecting karma. If you practice yoga and meditation and drink alcohol (yes, even that one cup of wine to be a "social drinker"), do drugs, are too much into negative thinking and eat meat, you have not stopped collecting karma. If you're

107

choosing to be on the path, do it the right way. When you do it the right way, you achieve your goal. Spirituality is something you can't pick and choose. How can you say you are spiritual, yet by actions are a hypocrite? How can you tell your children to never drink or smoke, yet you do it yourself?

Go about spirituality the right way with right guidance. Enlightenment and liberation will happen in your life when you are completely clear of karma and there are no more clouds. Start working on yourself now. Don't wait.

Even though I encourage you to live a nonviolent life, I will share with you a bitter truth: your physical existence is violence. You cannot escape being somewhat violent. When you breathe, you kill living beings. As you sit, walk, and talk, you are killing living beings. When you eat, something living had to be harmed or killed. Our mere existence is violence, and in order to survive we must commit some violence. However, Acharya Shree says, "We cannot be 100% nonviolent, but we can *minimize* the violence."

In order to survive, we must breathe, drink water, and eat, all of which contain living bacteria, fruits, or vegetables. Without them, we cannot live. For basic survival, we do not collect heavy karma that blocks our soul. In order to grow on the path, become enlightened and ultimately liberated, we do need to minimize the violence.

There are many forms of violence that can be discussed. For now, I will share with you what Acharya Shree has taught me over the years, which has the most violence (in our current society), so that you can consider to stop doing it, which means you've already minimized the violence and are not collecting karma.

**Eating Animals:** Vegetarianism is the first step of nonviolence. By becoming vegetarian or even vegan, you stop harming and killing animals in the name of diet. If you've ever watched videos from PETA or documentaries such as *Earthlings, Forks Over Knives, Vegucated, or Meet your Meat,* you will see how animals are treated—cruelly and inhumanely. You will hear their screams and see their blood splattered. It can be difficult to watch, but this is what happens. At the grocery store, meat is nicely packaged so you do not see the horror. When you eat meat, such as a burger or chicken fingers, you might be eating meat that has been mushed together from one hundred cows or chickens. That means they all had to die in order to make up the patty you might be eating.

Society promotes the meat diet for many reasons: It has become the accepted norm, it's abnormal to not eat meat, there are tons of myths that encourage meat eating (such as the

109

protein myth), big industries make a lot of profit from selling meat, the health issues you can get (like diabetes, high cholesterol, cancer), require you to take medication (which leads to profits in the pharmaceutical industry). If there are no illnesses, many doctors and researchers will not have a job. It's sad to say this, but many people make a profit from sickness and disease.

Even though the meat industry exists and they play the biggest role in killing animals, Acharya Shree says, "The one who eats the meat is the main killer." Why? Because if there were no demand for the meat in the first place, the meat industries could not exist. There is supply because there is demand. If there is no demand, no supply. If you had to kill the animal yourself, most probably you would not pull the trigger or slice its throat. It's difficult to kill and eat them when you look into their eyes.

Being a meat eater is a habit that was learned and it is considered normal. Maybe you cannot change your past, but you can change your future. Get healthy. Minimize the violence. Stop collecting karma. Be vegetarian.

**Alcohol & Drugs:** Alcohol and drugs are poison to the body. When you are under the influence you can cause violence. For example, if you drive and are under the influence of alcohol or drugs you can kill someone on the road because your awareness is completely impaired. When you drink and are angry, you might begin to be verbally, emotionally, and physically abusive. The same applies to drugs. Even if you do not consider yourself an alcoholic or use hard drugs, but consider yourself a social drinker or user, you are still polluting and being violent to your body. Minimize the violence and stop using it. If it is too hard to quit right away, at least start reducing the amount, and eventually, with time and deeper understanding, you can minimize and even stop all together. Any addiction, any craving, any desire brings karma. It is in your control. Work on yourself. Be a master of yourself.

**Hunting:** It is violence to eat an animal. It's even more violence to kill them by yourself, especially for sport. By taking the life of any living being, you collect karma.

You have to remember, each living being has a soul—just like you and me. At this time in their life cycle, they have an animal body. In their next life they could be a human and it may be your turn to have an animal life. Would you like some other human hunting you down and killing you? Of course not. You would live in fear and experience so much pain. If you are a hunter, leave behind your joy in hunting. Save an animal's life. Save your soul.

In today's society, an animal's life is not equal. What society forgets is that there are reasons why certain insects and animals are here. They have a purpose, just as we do. Their purpose is not to fill our stomachs. Maybe they remove the poisons from the earth, maybe they pollinate, maybe they help make the soil more fertile. The idea that the animal kingdom will overpopulate if we do not hunt and kill them is a myth. Mother Nature knows how to take care of herself. The problem is that humans interfere with nature too much and Mother Earth becomes imbalanced—why else are there tsunamis, tornadoes, hurricanes, fires, global warming? Humans have such a big ego that they think they know everything. You can't beat nature. Listen to nature. See that nature is trying to balance itself. Humans just keep ruining it. Don't take an animal's life. Let them die naturally. Let them fulfill their purpose. Who are we to interfere with a soul's evolution?

For the hunter, most of the major karma collected (so major that they can have an animal body or insect body in their next life), is because they celebrate their kill. It is one thing to kill an animal or to kill someone to protect your life. There is little to no karma in that because the intention is to defend and protect. However, if you kill an animal, take away its life, celebrate, and are proud of your success, you collect a lot of bad karma. Your intention was to kill, you killed, and then you got an ego (pride) about it, then you've just brought a whole lot of karma clouds to your soul. You might not see the suffering in this life, but karma always comes back to you, a thousand fold.

Acharya Shree established an ashram in Texas because he wanted to bring about the most change. In order to bring about big change, you go where it is the hardest to change. Texas is proudly known as a hunting and meat eating state. If one state can become totally nonviolent, the ripple effects of transformation will influence other states too.

**Big Lies:** No one likes big lies. Acharya Shree says that big lies collect more karma than the little lies. He always gives the example, "If someone is in court and the witness lies and says that someone is a killer even though they are not, that is considered a big lie." A big lie can destroy someone's life. It is better to live by truth always.

**Killing Living Beings:** It might be just a little bug, but this little bug also has a beautiful soul too. Out of habit or fear, it might be very easy to step on a spider or slap a mosquito that seems to fly around your arm. Habits, in the form of killing little bugs and insects, also bring you karma. Minimize the violence. Stop swatting.

Walk with awareness, sit with awareness, eat with awareness... really, do everything with awareness. If you don't have awareness you might unconsciously kill a living being. When you walk, always look at least three feet ahead of you. This way you can see if there is a bug or animal in the way and not hurt or kill it.

When you find a creature that somehow came into your home, save its life instead of killing it. All you have to do is grab a paper towel or cup, and then release them outside. They may have ended up in your home because they got lost. Or maybe you don't keep your house as clean as it should be. It's not their fault, therefore give them a second chance at life. When you have been lost and panicked, didn't you wish for help? Bugs want some help too, they just aren't able to ask.

Question: "What if ants attack my house?" Ants are everywhere and they have a purpose of living too. If you do not keep your house clean, or seal your house, or forget to clean up the crumbs after you ate some cake, the ants will somehow get in. Protect your home. There are natural ways to keep ants outside. You can also sweep the ants and place them outside far away from your home. Be innovative. Don't just step on them!

Awareness helps you to be compassionate, save lives, and

minimize violence. You can save many lives. Save theirs. Save yours.

Activity: Reflect and write.

What violence will you start minimizing from now on?

# :: MANTRAS & MALA ::

A mala is set of prayer beads mostly used for reciting, chanting, or mentally repeating mantras. A mala is helpful to have because it helps you focus more on the mantra and be wholeheartedly into it versus being worried about number counting and then losing track. Besides being a mantra repetition tracker, it can hold tremendous energy. This way when you wear it, you are always carrying positive and protective energy.

Malas can be made of different materials including rudraksha (a seed from a special fruit), beads (these are from trees grown in the Himalayas), tulsi, sandalwood, and lotus root to name a few. According to Acharya Shree, the

117

rudraksha malas hold the most energy if the beads are real. There are also different types of beads for the rudraksha. Rudraksha beads with fewer faces are considered more rare — they are more precious, hold more energy — therefore are more expensive. Common rudraksha beads have five faces.

When I was twenty years old, I wanted a mala to have before I was deployed to Iraq. To me it represented spirituality and commitment to my practices. I purchased my first mala, which was sandalwood, in Venice Beach, California. I remember walking down the Venice boardwalk on a sunny afternoon. To my left was the sparkling ocean, and in front of me were many small shops selling different T-shirts, incense, art, sage, fruits, vegetables, and clothing accessories, and I was listening to drum circles creating awesome music. I stopped at a vendor who had multiple malas. I wasn't experienced with malas. All I knew was that I wanted one. I picked up my sandalwood mala for $10 and wrapped it around my wrist — it felt nice.

I kept my sandalwood mala with me during my deployment. I hung it on my bedpost or kept it in my pocket. My mala was too small to wear. I remember the day I received my first rudraksha mala. It was from Acharya Shree.

In late April of 2005, I went back home to California for a

ten-day break. I enjoyed the opportunity to see and learn from Acharya Shree again. During my short trip I visited the ashram at least five times. The last time I saw him before returning to Iraq was during a satsang—a spiritual gathering —at his Riverside ashram. He gave an inspirational talk and subtly reminded me to stay strong through life's challenges, that hard times will pass, and to always be courageous. After the satsang was over, he left to his room and soon came back into the main room where we were all sitting. He had a little white envelope in his hand. He asked me to step outside. I remember my heart was pounding when he asked to speak with me. I was so sad that I had to say good-bye to him all over again and return to war the next day. The knot in my throat was hurting. All I wanted was to be under his guidance for the rest of my life. War kept me away from that. When outside he said to me, "I wanted to give you a gift. I already blessed it." I remember opening the envelope excitedly and there inside was a rudraksha mala. "Wear it. You will always be protected any time you are far away from me. Don't worry about dying. You will come back home. You will start your spiritual training soon." I had tears in my eyes. It was the greatest gift I had ever received. It was a mala, and most important, it was given to me by my guru. It hangs above my altar to this day.

I was excited about my mala and showed it to all my soldier-friends when I arrived back in Iraq. Some touched it and even held it in their hands. Little did I know that I was not supposed to do this—that's why I'm sharing this story with you. Don't make the same mistakes I did. If you have a mala, don't let anyone else touch it. Protect it. It's your energy and you have worked hard to create that energy. If someone touches it and by chance they are very negative, they can *zap* all the positive energy out of it. Acharya Shree says that a young child will not zap the mala because their minds are still positive and they are innocent. Always protect your mala and keep it in a safe place. Wear it under your blouse or shirt, close to you. Or keep it safe in your home somewhere that no one will find and touch it.

Along with protecting it and keeping it safe, it's also important to know how to properly use it. I didn't know how to use the mala when I first received it and actually practiced it incorrectly. Since elementary school, I was used to a Catholic rosary and assumed the way I used that rosary was the same way I should use the mala—thumb and index finger touching the bead. I was wrong. To use the mala properly, you should use the thumb and any other finger, except the index finger, to count the beads. I use my thumb and the inner part of my middle finger. The reason to not use the index finger is because energy-wise the index finger is used to suck and send energy. If the index finger is closed off, then all the positive energy you are creating doesn't get sucked as much into you. It is best not to use your index finger to count.

As a little tip for you: a good time to touch your index finger with your thumb together is when you are in a negative environment, surrounded by negative people, or in an argument. When you close your index finger with thumb, you will not suck the negative or hostile energy into you. Another good time to touch your index finger and thumb is when in meditation. By doing so, you create a simple *mudra*, *jnana* mudra, which generates energy and keeps the energy in you. It becomes a circuit of energy in your hands. Remember, more energy helps you enter meditation. Lastly, don't shower with your mala, because water will cause it to erode with time.

The mala normally consists of one hundred and eight beads. When you use your mala, always bring the beads towards you. It means you are bringing one hundred and eight spiritual qualities towards you. You always want qualities such as love, compassion, truthfulness, forgiveness, non-stealing, no-ego, non-possession, non-deceiving, giving, and patience to enter you. When you use your mala and send the bead out and away from you, you are getting rid of those qualities. Use your mala properly and you will gain the benefits.

You can use your mala for your spiritual practices any time —while you walk, sit, and stand. When you do your practices, do your best to recite any universal mantra at least one hundred and eight times (one full mala). If you would like to do more malas, reverse the beads and go backwards, keep reversing the direction until you decide to end.

If you don't have a mala or you would like a new one, you can order one at http://siddhayatan.org/store. You can request that your mala be blessed too.

ACTIVITY: Mantra recitation with mala.

Do one mala of the universal mantra, Arhum. Pronounce a-re-hung. If you do not have a mala, recite arhum one hundred and eight times out loud or mentally. If you feel like reciting more, do it. Practice and effort are never wasted on the spiritual path.

The mala is a helpful tool to help you with your spiritual practices, especially when doing either vocal repetition or mental repetition. I encourage you to use a mala—it is a reminder for you to always be spiritual, to be disciplined in your practices, and it provides protection as well.

# :: YOGA ::

When I started my journey of self-discovery at age seventeen, I was more interested in self-help books. The summer following my graduation, I stumbled upon a yoga studio called "Ahimsa Yoga" (ahimsa means nonviolence), and began taking classes there. This yoga studio was my entryway into eastern spirituality, beyond the popular self-help authors I was reading.

Ahimsa Yoga was fairly new when I first started attending. A full class those days had maybe three students. Most of my classes were private sessions, which I absolutely loved. I liked this yoga studio so much because it combined spirituality and philosophy. It wasn't a gym and it didn't showcase itself as a place of competition, ego, or yoga as merely an exercise. I was seeking something to enlighten my soul and help me to discover myself. When I was learning, my yoga teacher would combine positive affirmations with each posture. I really got into it: inhale peace, exhale worries. Inhale love, exhale anger. In tree posture: I am strong. I am calm. After each class, I remember feeling like I was on cloud nine. I would get into my car, put on some music by Enya, drive to the beach, embrace the sun's light, feel the wind on my skin, and I would smile. I felt so free. Yoga brought happiness into my life. Those days, yoga wasn't too popular—especially for an eighteen-year-old who was in search for truth and answers. My friends were more interested in hanging out. I was into finding myself. Yoga deepened my desire to search for my soul.

Yoga is an ancient discipline to purify and strengthen the body and mind to help you ultimately enter deep states of meditation and connect you to your deepest self. Yoga does not belong to any religion. The real yoga is spiritual in nature. It is not a fad. Real practitioners practice the eight-limb philosophy, which includes nonviolence, breathwork, concentration, meditation, plus other disciplines. It has deep teachings hidden in it. To learn about the true history of yoga, the yogic teachings before Pantanjali, and how it got corrupted over time, read *Chakra Awakening: The Lost Techniques* by Acharya Shree Yogeesh.

Shine Through Wisdom

I'm grateful that when I learned yoga it was from a good teacher who was doing his best to integrate the entire philosophy into his own life, especially nonviolence. It was from my first yoga teacher I learned vegetarianism is a must for any spiritual seeker. I also knew he was strict with his diet, didn't do any drugs, didn't drink alcohol, meditated daily, and you could see that peace reflected in his eyes. The only thing he couldn't do was guide me spiritually. He wasn't enlightened. He didn't have the answers I was seeking. I eventually found that guidance in Acharya Shree, but I'm grateful for my early yogic beginnings. Self-help authors helped me during my initial search for my higher self, yoga helped me get grounded and in touch with spirituality, and Acharya Shree took it to the next level and helped me totally transform and get fully on the spiritual path.

I remember when I informed my yoga teacher that I was going to US Army Basic Training I also asked if it would be possible to learn a sequence to help me prepare my body for the rigorous training I would have to go through. I was excited when he introduced the sun salutation. For me, my beginner classes consisted of very basic poses. I enjoyed each and every one of them and enjoyed mastering the simple postures. When I felt I was going to learn something more intensive and advanced, I was very excited. I always appreciated something that was challenging, because I knew I would have to push my body and mind, and with practice gain confidence that I could do more difficult things with my body.

The benefits of doing yoga are releasing stiffness, becoming more flexible, releasing toxins and tension that are in the bones and muscles, increasing circulation, and in general making the body stronger, lighter, and healthier. With a healthy and strong body, you can do a lot of spiritual practices for extended periods of time. When you have a strong and healthy body, you can burn your karma. When you have a disciplined body, you can enter meditation. One thing about spirituality is that everything works together. You cannot just focus on one aspect of spirituality and believe you will get enlightenment.

Remember, you need to achieve the three jewels of right knowledge, right vision, and right conduct. This happens with a healthy body, healthy mind, and awakened soul. Doing breathing alone is not enough. Doing mantras alone won't cut it. Reading only spiritual books doesn't bring you the knowledge you need. You need to work hard on yourself. Purify your body. Expel all those toxins. Create spiritual and positive energy around you. Remove your blockages. Dissolve your inner enemies. Go deep into meditation to realize yourself. Everything works together to help you know yourself. If you want to be more spiritual, know that you have to integrate multiple spiritual practices and disciplines to help you achieve your greatest goal—yourself.

Activity: Yoga.

Do the sun salutation three times. (You can find the sun salutation sequence online.)

Doing something every day is way better than reading about spirituality and doing nothing. Action burns karma. Collected knowledge doesn't. Make your body strong and healthy. Your soul is tired of being in the grip of karma.

Wake up. Wake up. Wake up.

# :: MANTRAS ::

Acharya Shree always says, "All of my teachings can be summed up in the Namokar mantra. It contains the science and system to liberate any soul. I can teach for days on this mantra."

The Namokar mantra is a universal mantra which embodies the complete spiritual path from beginning to end — from the practitioner to liberation. It helps you become humble, raise your energy, and it reminds you of your potential — liberation. This is a mantra I highly suggest you master.

"Namo" in Sanskrit means "I bow." Therefore this is the mantra for bowing, or humbleness. In order to crush your ego, you must bow. It is extremely difficult for anyone with a big ego to bow. Bowing shows your ability to be humble—to surrender. In the Namokar mantra, you are bowing to all siddhas (liberated souls), arihantas (living enlightened masters), acharyas (leaders of spiritual congregations), upadhyayas (spiritual teachers), and sadhus (female and male monks).

What I personally love about this mantra is that we are not paying respect to just anyone and not to a single individual, but rather bowing to all those who are truly on the spiritual path in the entire universe—the real path, not the religious one, not the pick and choose your own spirituality one, not the superficial one, but the real path that includes removing all karma and leads to liberation. Yes, that path.

If you can be in a room with all liberated souls, all arihantas of the past and future, with all spiritual leaders, with all spiritual teachers, and with all spiritual monks and nuns, wouldn't you be in awe, ecstatic, humbled, honored, and totally at their feet—literally? I would. This is what the mantra does for you. When you are wholeheartedly into this mantra, you create that divine and powerful energy as a result of this mantra, and then go deep into meditation and become in tune with all of them, you will burn your karma. It will burn, burn, burn. This mantra is very powerful. What is great is that it doesn't belong to any religion. Anyone can practice it. Anyone can free their soul.

The original Namokar mantra, which was taught by Enlightened Master and Tirthankara Adinath thousands and thousands of years ago, was *Namo Siddhaanam* (you learned this one earlier), and *Namo Arihantaanam*. This encouraged bowing to all enlightened masters and all liberated souls. Later, the other three—bowing to spiritual leaders, teachers, and practitioners—were added.

The Namokar mantra basically represents the five higher states of consciousness. Yes, when you are on the spiritual path you are considered very high. Now don't get ego-y on me. The reason you are considered high is because there are many living beings from bacteria all the way to humans who are far from thinking about spirituality at all. They are so immersed in the world, desires, pleasure, etc., that they don't even think to question who they really are and how to be free. In this aspect, for you to even consider working on yourself, knowing who you are and trying to realize the truth already shows that you are higher.

Acharya Shree defines a spiritual practitioner as one who is committed to non-violence, is vegetarian, is truthful, does not steal, does not hunt, does not do drugs or smoke or drink alcohol, does not gamble, does not engage in prostitution (those who voluntarily do it, not because they are abused and are forced to and trafficked by pimps). If you still do any of these things, drop them. Drop them for good. Be a real spiritual practitioner.

The Namokar mantra contains many seeds and also brings different colors of light and energy into the body including: white, red, yellow/orange, blue/green, and smokey black.

## THE NAMOKAR MANTRA

Namo Arihantaanam
Namo Siddhaanam
Namo Aairiyaanam
Namo Uvajjhaayaanam
Namo Loe Savva Saahunam

Eso Pancha Namokaaro
Savva Paavappanaasano
Mangalaanang cha Savvesim
Padhamam Havai Mangalam

**Namo Arihantaanam.** *(Na-mo aree-han-taa-nung)*
I bow to all enlightened masters.
Namo means bow. Arihantaanam means the Arihantas

(plural). Arihanta means an enlightened soul with a body. They have realized the highest states of consciousness, have removed all their heavy karmas, have attained right vision, right knowledge, and right conduct, and will then be completely liberated after the death of the body. The only difference between an enlightened master and a liberated soul is that they are still in their last body.

It's important to note that the Namokar says "Arihantas," which means there is not only one enlightened master in the universe. There are countless enlightened souls in other galaxies. By saying "Namo Arihantaanam," you are bowing to all the enlightened masters. Thus, you are humbling yourself and crushing your ego.

**Namo Siddhaanam.** *(Na-mo sid-dhaa-nung)*
I bow to the liberated souls, or I bow to God.
Siddhaanam means the Siddhas (plural) or liberated souls. The liberated souls have the same bliss as the arihantas, but the siddhas are bodiless. Thus, those who have entered moksha will never return, be reincarnated, or come back in human/ animal form. The siddhas are free from all suffering and pain.

You may wonder why the "Arihantas" are mentioned before the "Siddhas" since siddhas are without body. The reason is, the Arihantas still have a body and are able to share with us their bliss and enlightenment. You can be in tune with the siddhas; however, they cannot teach or communicate, but the arihantas can. That is why it is important to know a living enlightened master, the arihanta. I am so humbled, honored, and grateful to know Acharya Shree Yogeesh.

**Namo Aairiyaanam.** *(Na-mo aa-ee-ree-yaa-nung)*
I bow to the spiritual leaders.

Aairiyaanam (plural) are the leaders of the sangha. They are not fully enlightened yet, but are very close. At max, according to Acharya Shree, they are two to three lives away from being enlightened. Also, a soul can be at the level of consciousness of an Acharya and become an Arihanta in the same life.

**Namo Uvajjhaayaanam**. *(Na-mo uva-jai-yaa-nung)*
I bow to the spiritual teachers.

Uvajjhaayaanam (plural) are the spiritual teachers. They are very knowledgeable and are able to teach and express spiritual teachings. The knowledge comes from the experiences of their soul, and not from logic or books. They teach from their self-realization and higher state of consciousness.

**Namo Loe Savva Saahunam.** *(Na-mo lo-e sa-va saa-hu-nung)*
I bow to the female and male monks.

The monks noted in the Namokar mantra reflect all those who have taken the true step on the spiritual path, as I described before. You must know that this line does not refer to just any monk from any religion. This is beyond religion. It is about spirituality. Depending on their effort and karma, a monk can advance quickly to the state of enlightenment in the same life. These are rare cases, but it is not impossible. It depends whether or not the soul is ready.

**Eso Pancha Namokaaro Savva Paavapanaasano Mangalaanang cha Savvesim Padhamam Havai Mangalam**. *(Eso pan-cha na-mo-kaa-ro sa-va paa-va-pa-naa-sa-no mung-ga-laa-nam-cha sav-ve-sing pa-dha-mung ha-vay mung-ga-lung)*

This five-fold bowing down mantra completely destroys all karma. Among all auspicious mantras, this is the first and foremost.

The first five lines of the Namokar mantra are considered the main mantra. The last two lines describe what the Namokar mantra is and what it can do for you. Since you are a spiritual practitioner, you should recite this mantra which is the most important. You want to recite the mantra that helps destroy all karma. This mantra creates tremendous energy.

Activity: Mantra recitation.

Recite the first five lines (all the "namos") twenty-seven times.

Namo Arihantaanam
Namo Siddhaanam
Namo Aairiyaanam
Namo Uvajjhaayaanam
Namo Loe Savva Saahunam

Reflect and write.

In your journal, based on Acharya Shree's description of who is a true spiritual practitioner, what do you need to do to change and improve yourself to consider yourself a real practitioner? What do you need to let go of?

All spiritual practices and mantras are beneficial for your path—when you do them. As you get more into your practices and can dedicate more time, do your best to increase the amount of mantras you do per day. Make it a goal so that you are able to recite the five lines of the Namokar mantra one hundred and eight times per day. It might sound like a lot in the beginning, especially since you are learning the pronunciation, but with time and practice it will go quickly.

When I was in California, working full-time and going to

136

school full-time, I felt like I had no time whatsoever. Regardless, Acharya Shree told me I needed to do one mala every day. And so I did. When I first became a monk, my daily practice was six malas of the Namokar mantra, among other practices. It was a lot at first: a practice I wasn't used to. But eventually I got used it and began to enjoy it. When your practices mean the world to you, you will find the ten to twenty minutes in your day to dedicate to your self and your spiritual improvement.

# :: BRAHMACHARYA ::

Brahmacharya means to "always be in tune with God." That is the best way to live. Be in tune with your soul. Be in tune with God. Each and every moment. During a deep spiritual experience, a Tirthankara (an extraordinary kind of enlightened master on another planet), passed on the message to me once: Be active in your soul, day and night. This means that we should always be with and focus on our soul—in our thoughts, actions and speech, never wasting a single moment. Unfortunately, Brahmacharya has been translated as celibacy. And celibacy is often translated as "abstaining from sexual relations." According to Acharya Shree, celibacy is the incorrect translation. Brahmacharya really means: Be with your soul, always. I prefer that definition. Whether it is sex, lust, luxury, food, money, status, respect, or any other worldly desires and pleasures, we should not be taken away from our souls. No matter what. To become a monk, I took the vows of celibacy and Brahmacharya: A vow to always dedicate my life to soul and abstain from all desires.

Many religious and spiritual teachings use the popular definition, celibacy, as part of their practices or vows to become a monk or nun. The problem with this is that there is a lack of understanding. When you take a vow to abstain from marriage or sex only, it becomes more of a restraint. You have to control yourself. A "no, you can't do this." But there is no explanation behind it. That's why there are problems in major religions, like the Catholic Church. They take a vow of celibacy but do not have any deeper understanding except to accept it as a rule and vow in their life. That's why some (not all) have erred and have gone so far as to abuse children and adults. If you live with the real definition of brahmacharya, then there is no need to have "control of your senses." When you are with your soul, you cannot commit heinous crimes. You are rooted in deep spiritual understanding.

Brahmacharya is very important for you. Why? It's a reminder to stay away from anything, including sexual desires, which take you away from soul and pollute your mind. Controlling anything creates tension inside and makes it stronger than you. For example, the more you try to control your anger, the more your anger increases. It also hurts yourself and others. If you try to control your sexual desires, they become stronger. When you understand this spiritual teaching, you are relaxed and there is nothing to control.

In my early years as a monk and even here and there today, many approach me: "You don't want any children? You do not want to get married? Do sexual thoughts ever cross your mind?"

I always answer, "No."

Soul is my number one priority. Liberation is my number one goal. I want to free myself of all my chains. I only want soul. I don't want to create anymore chains, responsibilities, attachments, and I also don't want to fall off the path. Any desire, even small, can easily take you off the path, especially if it gets very strong. That's why we have to close all the open sources. Say no to all desires, not just one. If you don't feed it, it cannot bother you.

My elementary school principal, Sr. Ena, is a Catholic nun. She has known me since I was five years old and attended Catholic elementary school. Fortunately, she is very open-minded and has supported my spiritual journey—even though it is outside Catholicism. We are quite close and when I visit California, I'm always welcome to stay at the convent (living community for nuns), which I always do for a few nights. One morning as we were having breakfast, she asked me out of the blue (with her Irish accent), "Siddhali, you know, you are thirty. You are in your prime age. I know that to become a nun you took the vow of celibacy. Has it been challenging for you?" I was shocked to hear the question coming from her. I've been asked so many times, but when you are asked if you have sexual thoughts by your elementary school principal-turned-spiritual friend, who has been a Catholic nun for many years, it shocks you a bit. I told her the same thing I said before. "Sr. Ena, I'm thirty, yes, but those temptations are not there for me. I know my path. This is what I want. I don't want anything else or anyone to distract me." It was interesting to hear her ask me this question because it is something many nuns and priests have difficulty with. Maybe common, but unspoken.

Sex is part of the spiritual discussion. Acharya Shree says that if you are on the spiritual path, you need to have a good understanding about it. He advises not to be promiscuous and have many partners. If you are married, do not have any sexual relations outside of your marriage. If you do, it brings karma to you for your deceitfulness and because your desires are so strong. If you are unmarried, do not sleep around. The spiritual path requires a lot of energy to help you advance on your path and go deep into meditation. When you have sex, you lose that energy, especially when you have multiple partners. Try to find someone who is on the same spiritual level as you, this way you do not lose your energy. To deepen your understanding about sex and spirituality consider watching one of our popular YouTube videos:

https://www.youtube.com/watch?v=I_vjaTDaOaA

In the self-help world, there is a lot of mention of "self-love." I support self-love. By loving myself I started my spirituality journey. Unfortunately, some have misinterpreted self-love to include servicing yourself, masturbation. When you masturbate, you also lose a lot of energy. Don't get confused. Remember, the focus of your path is to know your self and know your soul, not enhance and feed the pleasures and cravings of your body and mind. The more you do the techniques and practices mentioned in this book, the more the toxins will leave. The more toxins leave you, the less the polluted mind has control over you. When you have understanding and the real spiritual teachings become clear for you, changing yourself and habits are not that hard. When on the spiritual path, you are determined to know the soul and not focus on anything else that takes you away from it. Your desires and cravings, regardless of what they are, bring you karma. Stay away from them. Improve yourself. Raise yourself higher. Protect your path.

Activity: Reflect and write.

What strong desires do you currently have that take you off the path? What desires keep you away from being active in your soul, day and night?

Brahmacharya is not limited to abstaining from sex. It means to abstain from everything that keeps you away from soul. If you have the thought, "Well, life's going to be boring without the little pleasures. What else am I going to do?" It shows you need to deepen your understanding of soul. Practice Brahmacharya. Be active in your soul, day and night. Never waste a single moment being taken from your soul. Pain and pleasure belong to the world. Break free from your chains. That should be your ultimate goal. Strive for bliss.

# :: THE PRESENT MOMENT ::

When I bought my own car at age seventeen, I was finally able to enjoy spontaneous adventures. I enjoyed having the random thought pop in my head that said, "Hey, go to the beach! Take your favorite drive. Drive through the hills of San Pedro and Palos Verdes, and end up at Redondo Beach. Enjoy a cup of coffee. Go to the theatre and watch a movie by yourself." And then I would go do it. I loved living in the moment.

I remember when I was a senior, we had a day off from school, and one of my close friends called me at 6:00 am. "Hey, what are you doing today?" "I dunno, I'm up for whatever." Then we got the crazy idea to drive three hours away with two more friends and go to Big Bear Mountain where it was snowing. It was incredibly fun. We had no money, except for gas and snacks. We were far away from our homes and our parents. We felt we were in another world. We played in the snow. I brought my journal and sat on a big rock in the snow. I felt like I was a *big time writer*, writing in a beautiful scene of nature, where all my thoughts and emotions easily flowed on to the paper. My other friends were sitting and chatting amongst themselves about the purpose of life and sharing their hopes and dreams. We walked around the snow-covered trees. We had snowball fights. It was the most unexpected adventure. It was unplanned. It was liberating.

Now of course, when I got home and was asked by parents where I was, I got yelled at. My actions were irresponsible. I didn't ask to go three hours away and to a mountain. That was expected. Despite getting screamed at, my heart was still smiling. I was happy. I always loved and appreciated spontaneity—the smiles and laughs from those moments can never be forgotten. That Big Bear adventure was over thirteen years ago and it's still fresh in my mind.

When we are stuck or taken by the past or future, we are far away from soul. It shows we are in the mind. If you are constantly living in the past—thinking about past memories, past regrets, past relationships, past mistakes, etc.—you are what Acharya Shree calls, "living in the mind without meaning." When you are living in the past, you could be living in regret, guilt, stress, depression.

The same thing applies to the future. When you live in the future, you live in nervousness, worry, anxiety, stress, and fear. You live in imagination, fantasy, hope, and anticipation. Anything that is over planned creates stress. There are too many expectations in over planning, which can lead to disappointment. Over planning shows you live in fear and control. Remember, you cannot control any one, any event, or any thing. It is good to plan, but be comfortable, flexible, and allow things to flow.

When you live in the past and future, there is hardly any room for adventure. If you are too much into the future and planning for it, it seems like you are living a scripted life. Have fun a little. Don't take life so seriously. Live!

It is best to live moment to moment.

I always give this example when I am talking with students:

You are walking in the desert under the hot sun. You are thirsty and tired. Yet you look behind you and you have been dragging this large cart filled with baggage. The baggage is filled with too many items-clothes, pictures, memories, worries, etc. For the entire journey that you've been walking in the desert, you've been dragging this cart. You are out of energy. The journey is taking forever to complete. All you have to do is let go. Let go of the cart. Let go of the baggage. Let go of all the negativities from your past. Your journey will become much lighter. When you let it go, you can get to your destination much faster. Why carry the past with you into today? It serves no purpose. Get rid of it.

The mind is very powerful, it plays tricks on you, and can be quite convincing. Things that do not even exist can be believable if the mind gets too strong. The mind doesn't want you to know soul. It wants to be in control of you. It wants power over you. No wonder the soul is so weak. We have always paid attention to the mind, and not the soul. We put trust in the fluctuating and inconsistent mind, and not in the infinite, all-knowing soul. We can change this when we live moment to moment.

When we live moment to moment or in the present moment, we live in soul. When you are in soul, you flow. It's easier to flow with the river than fight and resist it. When you live in the moment you are living with awareness.

When you live with awareness you will immediately notice

when mind, ego, anger, jealousy, greed, deceitfulness, violence, etc., come to the surface. Because of that awareness, your soul becomes stronger and becomes less and less affected by the mind. You can shift your thinking away from negativity to positivity when you live in the moment. If you are captivated by the mind—the past and the future—you cannot live and act from soul awareness.

The goal of spirituality is to give back strength to your soul. Even though the soul has infinite power, it is presently weak and under the control of the mind and senses. By living in the moment, living in flow, living in a relaxed way, and living with awareness, the soul can begin to get stronger and thrive. Soul is so desperate to get away from all the chains. It is tired of the karmic pollution. Don't feed or succumb to the mind by living in the past or the future. Stop creating stress for yourself. Stop thinking too much!

Stress can kill you. When you live in soul, you cannot live in stress. You might have a lot of things going on, but all those things do not kill you. You handle life and the responsibilities in a balanced way. When you are in mind and in stress, you can't enjoy life. When you work, work in a relaxed way. When you are relaxed, you will be more productive, have no stress, be more innovative and creative, and will you have much more focus.

Always live in the present moment. It is the only time that exists. The past doesn't exist and neither does the future. Just now. So be in the now.

ACTIVITY: Live in the present.

Do something super spontaneous today. Be weird. Take a little risk. Be different. Be you.

# :: SILENCE ::

Our ability to speak can be our best friend and worst enemy. As a best friend, our speech can bring us peace, joy, great friends, job opportunities, and much more. As an enemy, it uses abusive language, hurts, and can even kill others. The words we speak need to be watched. It is important to know the significance of watching your words, silence as a spiritual practice, and how to speak with purpose.

Because we have collected good karma, we are born with a body that has the ability to talk and express itself clearly. When we look at animals, their ability to communicate is limited, but the human body can speak its mind. Our ability to communicate is an instrument, but the languages learned and how we use our instrument are learned from our society.

There are three main ways to collect good and bad karma: through thoughts, actions, and speech. Used properly, speech can be used to unite, bring peace in the family, attract friends, and much more. Used improperly, it will attract enemies, hurt others, and collect bad karma.

Also, speech can be used in a negative way by using abusive language, whether they are bad words or words used with bad intentions to hurt others. Speech can also be used to gossip, talk behind another's back, lie, and much more. Such negative uses of the instrument of speech collect bad karma.

Many people have the habit of talking without necessity and some have a very strong habit that they do not know how to stop talking. This is a result of hyperactivity and scattered energy, which takes a person away from true stillness and peace.

Silence, in its true spiritual meaning, is to be completely silent from mind, thoughts, and emotions. Even though we use our instrument to speak, we can still be inwardly silent—this is very difficult to practice. That is why some people go on silent retreats to physically become quiet, with a hope to go beyond their mind and emotions and enjoy stillness.

If you are able to practice silence and not speak for one whole day (twenty-four hours), once or twice a month, you will learn how to dissolve your ego and thoughts, and become very humble. Also, by practicing silence, because speech is not in use, you cannot collect bad speech karma.

If becoming silent for one day is not possible, try to reduce the amount of speaking you do throughout the day. Instead of gossiping, chatting about things that are not important, and wasting energy, be silent for the moment. Speaking is a difficult habit to break for many, but it is a good discipline to incorporate into your sadhana. The less you speak, the more your words mean something.

That is why enlightened masters just speak to share the message, but afterwards they do not talk. They only say what you need to hear. They use their instrument with a purpose. You won't hear them chatting on the phone for three hours without meaning.

I like to practice "talking with meaning" myself and practice days of silence on occasion. I am very quiet at the ashram. I listen more and say few words. But, when it's time to talk about spirituality, or I need to inspire someone, or it's time to give a speech, it flows.

153

A few years ago I took a vow of silence. Every Sunday, for one whole year, I was in silence. It was the greatest gift I ever gave to myself.

Activity: Be silent and still.

Practice silence for a day. Or take a few hours out of your day to schedule silence. You can do it before work for one to two hours as you get ready, being aware not to make a single sound. If by mistake you speak, catch yourself and return to your silence. Silence and awareness takes time — eventually you will get used it. Flow with it. Don't resist it.

By practicing silence, you begin to train your physical body to not waste energy. As you practice silence, you begin to notice your emotions and thoughts more. Once you start gaining awareness, you will begin to silence your emotions and thoughts and go beyond them. After practicing silence with your emotions and thoughts, you will then be able to enter into the silence of your soul. When you hear the silence, your heart will skip a beat because it is so beautiful, wonderful, and blissful.

# :: CHAKRAS, PART I ::

There are many tools to help you grow on the spiritual path. You've learned about yoga, meditation, breathing techniques, and mantras, along with important spiritual teachings. Another way to work on yourself is to work on your chakras. The chakras are seven wheels of energy that are located in your body—though they are not something you can touch with your hands, they do exist. The chakras help make up your aura, your energy field, which consists of different colors. They affect your physical, emotional and mental health. When your chakras are blocked, underactive, or overactive, they produce negative results in different aspects of your life. When your chakras are open, balanced, and active, you will encounter many spiritual benefits.

Sadhvi Siddhali Shree

The chakra system is a vast subject and includes many teachings, concepts, and techniques. Acharya Shree Yogeesh published a comprehensive book on the chakras titled: *Chakra Awakening: The Lost Techniques*, which covers the history of spirituality, the misconceptions and false teachings of yoga and the chakras, and lost techniques of chakra activation that have not been practiced for over 2900 years. If you like the chakras, are very curious, or would like to learn new spiritual practices, I highly suggest you study Acharya Shree's book in-depth.

For now, you will get a basic overview of the chakras and basic chakra activation.

There are seven energy centers throughout the body and they affect our physical, emotional, mental, and spiritual health. There is a certain energy, called the kundalini, which is a passage of energy that begins from the base of the spine to the top of your head. The seven chakras are located inside this kundalini passage.

The goal of chakra work, as a spiritual practice, is to make your energy strong and help your energy flow upwards. It is important to have energy flowing upwards, because this is the same energy that must be focused (through the power of concentration) to help you dive deep into your consciousness.

For example, in order for a skyrocket to propel into the infinite sky, it needs fuel for power. Likewise, energy is the fuel to propel you into soul. Not just any kind of energy, but pure, positive, and focused energy. When you are in any kind of negativity, your energy is low and scattered. If you are confused and seem lost in your thoughts, your energy is scattered. How do you expect to know and experience your soul if your energy is scattered all over the place? That is why we have to always work on ourselves. Everything is connected. When you work on your body, your mind, your energy, your chakras, it all helps you to know yourself more.

I was walking with a student after he had taken the Chakra Awakening Retreat at Siddhayatan. He asked me, "In theory I can understand what the chakras are and what they do. But c'mon, how does chakra work really help me in my life? Especially in my business?" I replied, "Any tool is helpful for the spiritual path if it is used and practiced. When you are balanced and centered you can handle any life situation that comes your way—whether in personal or business life." I continued, "If you have a weak second chakra, you will constantly live in fear. You might live in fear that your business will fail. You might feel unsettled and never comfortable, which reflects lack of confidence in your business, and much more. The whole idea of working on your chakras is to help you get through each day in a balanced and energetic way. If they help you increase energy, focus, trust in yourself, fearlessness, and give you clarity for your personal, spiritual, and business life, why not use them?" He understood and went on to his next question.

In this section you will learn about the first three chakras and in the next, you will learn about the last four.

## FIRST CHAKRA

The first chakra is the Muladhara. It is located at the base of the spine and its color is red. If you want to meditate on this chakra, visualize red to help begin activation. Its element is earth.

The goal is to have a balanced, activated, and awakened chakra. When the first chakra is awakened, you will be full of energy, grounded, productive, and have overall good health. If your first chakra is blocked and not balanced, some of the symptoms you might feel are being tired, lazy, sick, or diseased. If your chakra is overactive, then you will feel hyper and scattered.

The rate at which the chakra, wheel of energy, spins determines if a chakra is active, overactive, underactive or blocked. When a chakra spins too fast or too slow, it brings negative results. The goal of working on your chakras is to bring them to a balanced state.

Many guests who have come to the Chakra Awakening Retreat at Siddhayatan often have a blocked or overactive first chakra. Sometimes someone's first chakra will be 60-70% blocked, and Acharya Shree will ask how they are even alive. Having a healthy first chakra is key to healthy living and leading a highly spiritual life. You need energy, you need fuel, to grow.

The role of the first chakra is to generate energy. If this chakra is blocked or closed it can be harmful to you. The first chakra also helps you stay grounded, centered, and focused in life. Unfortunately, many meditation and yoga teachers have their students focus solely on the sixth chakra, also known as the "third-eye." When you focus on the sixth chakra while your first chakra is blocked or inactive, you will not have much energy to use to help you enter states of meditation. However, if you have energy in your first chakra, then when the energy flows up, you will have energy to use for meditation when concentrating. Many people try to jump to the top of the ladder, especially with meditation. But it's important to build your chakra foundation starting from the root up. Why do people meditate for a long time without any experiences? Because they do not have much energy. You must focus and awaken your first chakra first, to help you achieve your spiritual goals.

It's very common for people who are working on improving themselves, awakening their souls, and even activating their chakras, to lose all the energy they have created. When you get angry, depressed, jealous, or have lower qualities, the energy from the chakras begin to flow downwards and you begin to lose all that energy. People feel down because they have no energy in their chakras. When you are positive, your energy begins to rise. So it's important to be positive in order to retain the energy you have created. Another way to lose energy in your first chakra is by being promiscuous and having multiple sex partners. When you are married or in love with someone and express that love, you are sharing energy with them. But if you are having sex with random people who aren't on the spiritual path at all or have negative energy or you do not care about, they can suck out all the energy you've worked so hard to generate. So be careful, for your health and chakra's sake. Protect yourself.

Like all mantras, it is important to learn the correct way to pronounce the activation sounds. Especially with Prakrit or Sanskrit, accurate pronunciation is important because it is the divine sound that is helping you. It is specific energy that is being created. If you say it incorrectly, it can bring you negative results.

The chakra activation sound for the first chakra is *lam*. It is pronounced like "lung." When you are activating your chakra, visualize red light at the base of your spine and recite out loud: lam lam lam. Repeat at least twenty-seven times daily.

You can hear the correct pronunciation of all the chakra activation sounds mentioned in this book at http://shinethroughwisdom.com/mantras. For chakra guided meditations, I co-created a cd, *7 Chakra Guided Meditations*, which you can get a copy of at http://siddhayatan.org/store. This cd contains peaceful music, a guided meditation, and activation sounds for each chakra.

The benefits of activating the first chakra include generating vital energy in the body, becoming centered and grounded, becoming healthier, creating energy for spiritual advancement, and most important, focusing and nurturing your "roots." Muladhara itself means "root." That's why you have to take care of your roots so you can blossom. If you merely pay attention to the branches and leaves at the sixth chakra, it won't help you grow. If you focus on your roots, you will grow. Be patient with your growth. Build a strong spiritual foundation. You will blossom.

## SECOND CHAKRA

The second chakra, Svaadhisthaan, is located two inches up from the base of your spine. Its color is orange and if you want to meditate on this chakra, visualize orange to help begin activation. Its element is water.

When the Svaadhisthaan chakra is awakened, you will be confident, fearless, secure with yourself, and protected. If your second chakra is blocked and not balanced, some of the symptoms you might feel are being insecure, impatient, irritable, fearful, feeling inferior, and having no peace of mind. If your chakra is overactive, you will feel sensitive and overcome with sexual desire.

The role of the second chakra is your overall sense of security. This chakra helps you feel at home with yourself, comfortable, confident, and free of anxiety and worry. We live in a demanding society that makes most people uncomfortable with who they are and, in worst cases, dislike or hate themselves—which is violence. We are inundated with ads that promote a certain look, weight, or fashion, making many people unhappy with who they are. When your second chakra is awakened, you will be confident and happy with yourself as you are. Loving the real you. Do not stress yourself out trying to meet the demands and expectations of your parents, others, or society. Be yourself. Love yourself. Believe in yourself. Deep down most people want the freedom to be their true selves. Do it. Balance your second chakra and you will see the positive difference in your life.

The activation sound for the Svaadhisthaan chakra is *vam*. It is pronounced as "vung". Visualize orange light two inches above the base of your spine and recite: vam vam vam. Repeat it at least twenty-seven times daily.

The benefits of activating the second chakra include creating energy in the body, adding orange color to your aura, becoming healthier, creating energy for spiritual advancement, feeling secure with yourself and others, and being confident and fearless. If you have ever experienced fear while going deep into meditation and the unknown, when you balance this chakra, the fear will become less and less. There is nothing to fear when discovering the depths of your soul.

## THIRD CHAKRA

The third chakra, Manipura chakra, is located in the center of your body—at your navel. "Mani" means "jewel." When energy flows to this center, you become like a jewel. You are a diamond. The color of this chakra is yellow and the element is fire.

When your energy moves up and your third chakra is awakened, you will be connected to and feel oneness with yourself, others, and the universe. You will be more intuitive and trust your gut. If your Manipura chakra is blocked, you will be doubtful, imbalanced, and have digestive problems. If your third chakra is overactive you will be aggressive, and have violent thoughts and emotions. Remember to never waste your time in anger, violence, fighting, jealousy, and hate. Those are low qualities that bring your energy down and make you scattered. Those qualities need to be dissolved and you need to transform.

It's important to know that whatever food you eat and digest affects your third chakra. Heavy foods will slow down this chakra. It is best to eat light foods for your chakra's (and health's) sake.

When your third chakra is awakened, it plays a big role in your life. You will be balanced, not live in duality, be connected to the universe, trust and know yourself, and be healthy through diaphragmatic breathing. Balance is key to spiritual awakening.

The activation sound for the Manipura chakra is *ram*. It is pronounced as "rung." To activate this chakra visualize yellow light at your navel and recite: ram ram ram. Repeat a minimum of twenty-seven times.

When you activate your Manipura chakra, the benefits are: creating vital energy in the body, creating yellow color in your aura, increasing your metabolism, regulating your digestion, uplifting your energy for spiritual advancement, and trusting yourself and others. When you live from the third chakra, you are completely balanced. Whether someone criticizes you or praises you, you are completely unaffected. All the masters and saints live from this chakra. They are jewels, priceless, and live in inactivity. You can become a master too, when you become totally balanced in all aspects of your life, transform and awaken yourself.

Activity: Chakra activation.

Recite activation sounds for the first, second, and third chakras at least one hundred and eight times each. I highly suggest in enrolling in my complimentary video training I created on the chakras. You will receive pdfs and audio meditations which include reciting the chakra activation sounds. As of the writing of this book, fifteen thousand three hundred and seven people have already participated. You can sign up for the training at http://awakenchakras.com/freetraining.

Chakras play an important role in your life. When the chakras are balanced you are healthy, peaceful, calm, trusting, confident, energetic, and intuitive. Include chakra activation as part of your daily spiritual practices for at least forty-one days. Use the chakra activation tools to help awaken yourself.

It's your time.

Never waste a moment.

Shine your light.

# :: CHAKRAS, PART II ::

All chakras benefit you physically, mentally, and spiritually. It is important to first focus on the lower chakras to create a strong energetic foundation and then slowly start working on your upper chakras. The goal of your spiritual path is to always grow more and more. In the same way, you always want your energy to rise higher and higher.

The first of the upper chakras is the Anaahata chakra, the fourth chakra. In Sanskrit, "Anaahata" means the "soundless sound." Once you've balanced and awakened your lower three chakras and the energy rises, it will touch the fourth chakra which is located very close to your heart. The Anaahata chakra is green, so when you meditate, focus your attention at your heart and visualize green color. Its element is air.

When your energy has reached the fourth chakra and is awakened, you will experience unconditional love, devotion, have emotional balance, and become very compassionate. If your Anaahata chakra is blocked, you will be selfish, possessive, and unfriendly. If your fourth chakra is overactive, then you will have suffocating love and experience obsession.

The role of the fourth chakra is to help create and bring love and peace into your life. It will help transform your negative emotions into positive. It will heal the pain you carry with you. You will be able to forgive yourself and others. And most important, you can share your unconditional love without expectation of any love in return.

The activation sound for the Anaahata chakra is *yam*. It is pronounced like "yung." To activate your fourth chakra, visualize green light at the heart and repeat: yam yam yam at least twenty-seven times.

By activating this chakra, you will create green color in your aura, and open up your heart. People are hurt emotionally. Words often hurt more than wounds. So when you begin to work on this chakra and you've held on to or suppressed your emotions, do not be surprised when all the emotions, like anger, come up to the surface. Let your emotions out. It's okay. It may even create chaos. But after chaos and no more suppression, peace and love prevail. As a result, you will be able to experience oneness with all living beings. Increase your compassion. Dissolve more emotions. Connect with your soul. Hear the soundless sound.

One meditation technique Acharya Shree taught me was to focus on my heart, create awareness, then listen to my heartbeat. Once you can hear your heartbeat, the chance may come where you can jump into real meditation. When you jump into meditation, then you will hear the soundless sound. It's not easy to listen to your heartbeat, especially with so much noise to distract you, but if you are able to do it, it shows your concentration power, your ability to focus and listen, which are required to enter states of deeper meditation. You need to tune out the world to be able to tune in.

Try it one day.

### FIFTH CHAKRA:

The Vishuddhi chakra is located at your throat. The chakra's color is sky blue. So whenever you want to activate it during meditation, visualize sky blue at your throat. The element is bone. This is an important chakra to always keep active and balanced—it is all about expression.

When your fifth chakra is balanced and awakened, you will be creative, hear your inner voice, communicate with clarity, and be bold. If your fifth chakra is blocked you will be shy and have difficulty expressing yourself, whether it's your thoughts or emotions. If you have an overactive fifth chakra, you have trouble listening to others, a hard time comprehending what you listen or read, and may be talkative. You may have come across a person who is very talkative and you do not know how to respectfully stop them. It shows they have an overactive fifth chakra.

The role of the fifth chakra is very important, especially with the thymus gland. When the thymus gland is weak, you will be lazy, tired, have poor blood circulation, problems with your lungs, experience other health issues, and have no energy at all. Many take medication because this gland is not balanced and prevents the body from functioning correctly. In extreme cases, when this gland is weak, people can even die. So having a balanced and awakened fifth chakra is critical.

The Vishuddhi chakra's role includes being your communication center, your source of creative expression, as well as bringing you calmness.

The chakra activation sound is *ham*. It is pronounced as "hung". Visualize sky blue color at your throat and meditate on this visualization while repeating hum hum hum at least twenty-seven times.

The benefits of awakening the Vishuddhi chakra are creating vital energy in the body, increasing sky blue color in your aura, having clear vocal and creative expression, always having the ability to listen and understand others, bringing calmness into your life, and getting in touch with the depths of your soul.

## SIXTH CHAKRA

The sixth chakra, Ajna, is the wisdom center and it is located at the point between your eyebrows. It is popularly known as the "third-eye." When you meditate and focus on the Ajna chakra, try to visualize indigo. It governs over the subtle bodies.

When your sixth chakra is awakened, all of your channels are open, meaning your body is healthy and mind is healthy. As a result you will experience spiritual awakening, have wisdom and right vision. If your sixth chakra is blocked, you will experience confusion, have no clarity, and won't have the ability to concentrate. If your Ajna chakra is overactive, then you will experience hallucinations, have too much imagination, and experience fantasizing and day dreaming. Remember that fantasy belongs to the future. Future creates anxiety or wishful thinking. Always live in the present moment. Keep your awareness there.

The role of the sixth chakra is very, very important, especially for spiritual advancement. As I mentioned before, most meditation and yoga teachers ask you to focus on the sixth chakra without teaching you to develop your first five chakras first. You need to have a lot of energy from the lower chakras to help you concentrate and visualize at this center, which can lead you towards meditation. When you are able to be in a thoughtless state, then you are in meditation. Remember, the more you *try* to meditate, the more you create tension. The more you pay attention to your thoughts, the more you will create tension that prevents you from entering meditation. Learn to let go. Be relaxed. Have no tension. That's when meditation can happen. And that's when you can have direct experience of the soul.

When there is acceptance, there is no resistance. When there is no resistance, there is no tension and stress. You are in total flow with soul.

There is a safe activation sound for the Ajna chakra. I say the word "safe" because you can recite these activation sounds without much concern for harming your chakras. There are powerful divine sounds that can be used to awaken your chakras, and if they are misused, they can do more harm than good. That's why it's important to be under right guidance, like under a living enlightened master, to learn the right sounds, how to say them, how many times to say them, and when it is time to stop.

The safe activation sound is *aum*, pronounced "om." Close your eyes, visualize indigo color at the point between your eyebrows and recite: aum aum aum. Repeat at least twenty-seven times.

The activation benefits of having an awakened sixth chakra helps you advance spiritually, have meditation experiences, get glimpses of soul, and the ability to know the truth (which is beyond intellect and logic). With a balanced Ajna chakra, negative thoughts will not attack you, you are positive most of the time, you gain clarity, work well, don't get tired, and receive never-ending soul knowledge.

The Ajna Chakra, when awakened, can reveal many secrets to you, when you go deep.

## SEVENTH CHAKRA

The final chakra is the Sahasrara chakra, which is located at the top of your head. Its color is pink (or white) and it has no elements.

When this chakra is awakened, you will experience bliss, ecstasy, spiritual visions, higher intuition, and the highest states of consciousness. When your seventh chakra is blocked, you will be rigid in your thinking and even prejudiced. When the Sahasrara chakra is overactive, you will have no concern for yourself or others, as well as no interest or effort towards spiritual awakening.

With all the energy flowing and rising upward, starting from your first chakra all the way to the top of your head, once it hits your seventh chakra, you can begin to experience ecstasy and bliss in meditation. The symbol of the Sahasrara is a thousand-petaled lotus. This means as you blossom, all the layers of your karma begin to break. When this chakra is completely active, it can lead you towards enlightenment.

The role of your seventh chakra is to help you advance spiritually, help you totally transform your life, and connect you to your soul's infinite knowledge.

The activation sound for the seventh chakra is similar to the sixth chakra. The safe activation sound is aum. However, you will pronounce *aum* in a different way. There will be an emphasis on the *m*. So when you emphasize the "m" you will feel the top of your head vibrate. Listen carefully to the activation sound at http://shinethroughwisdom.com/mantras. Always keep in mind the stress of the "m" when activating your seventh chakra and do not confuse it with the Aum from the sixth chakra.

By activating and awakening the Sahasrara chakra, you will begin to realize and awaken your soul and move towards enlightenment. Remember that all of your chakras have to be balanced and awakened for energy to start rising up. As you continue working on yourself by improving your thoughts, transforming your lower qualities into higher qualities, doing sadhana or spiritual practices to remove karma, as well as keeping your chakras balanced, you will move towards enlightenment.

Activity: Chakra activation.

Recite each activation sound for chakras four through seven at least one hundred and eight times each.

Work hard on yourself if you want to attain self-mastery

and the highest states of consciousness. Balance your chakras and you will become healthier physically, emotionally, mentally and spiritually. Your effort will be worth it in the end as you taste bliss. Bliss is eternal. Once you achieve it, it stays with you forever. Bliss is always new. It is the essence and nature of who you are.

# :: SPIRITUAL SPACE ::

Living in a spiritual environment helps you to be surrounded by peace, positive energy, calmness, but most important, it reminds you to be dedicated to the spiritual path. You might never live at an ashram or monastery during your lifetime, or live with monks to remind you to do your spiritual practices, but it doesn't mean you cannot have a spiritual environment in your own home.

I encourage you to create a *spiritual space* in your home. A spiritual space is a special spot in your home where you can do your spiritual practices. It is your go-to area when you feel overwhelmed, stressed, or angry. As soon as you are in your spiritual space you automatically begin to feel more peaceful, less stressed, and more calm. Your spiritual space is the location where you do a majority of your spiritual practices. And, when you are walking around in your house and glance at your spiritual space, it will remind you to do your practices.

By creating a spiritual space and doing your spiritual practices there, you create a bubble of positive, healing, and spiritual energy through your meditation, yoga, mantra, and other practices. Since this is a sacred spot for you, it is best to not to let others go near it.

A spiritual space can be as large as a room in your house, or it can be located in a corner of your bedroom. In your spiritual space, you can set up a small table and have candles, incense, and pictures of people who inspire you to be spiritual on it. Even though I live at an ashram and there are many places to do my spiritual practices, I have a spiritual space in my room. On my small table I have a picture of Acharya Shree, two small statues, candles, a painting someone gave to me, a rock I picked out of the Ganges River in India, and a quotation that says, "Those who care teach." When I'm not wearing my mala, I leave it on my small table. Inside my table are some of my journals. My room's spiritual space is pretty simple, however, it is my personal reminder to do my spiritual practices.

Here's a picture:

Some tips for setting up your spiritual space:

~ Always keep it clean and free of dust
~ Use a room divider to separate it from your bedroom
~ Setup a yoga mat and meditation pillow there
~ Include a picture of your spiritual master or teacher
~ Make sure your space doesn't face South
~ Do not let negative people touch your spiritual space

Sadhvi Siddhali Shree

It's easy to get caught up in life and all of its responsibilities, that is why we need to create reminders, such as a small space and an environment to help us stay on track. Creating a spiritual space reminds you to stay disciplined. It becomes a sacred refuge in your home, and it provides you with a bubble of positivity and energy whenever you need it.

With the spiritual teachings, techniques, and practices you have learned, you will now need to create a space where you can practice. It becomes your mini-ashram. Ashram means "place of spiritual learning and practices."

Activity: Create a spiritual space.

Decorate a room or small space in your home where you can do your spiritual practices. Set it up in a way that it inspires you to always be on the spiritual path.

# :: MEDITATION ::

To be in meditation means to be totally in flow, in the present moment, completely relaxed—a state of effortlessness. When you fully let go of your body and relax, you will be able to bypass your mind, and once the mind is far away from you, you are with yourself, soul.

I was conducting a meditation retreat and at the beginning of the second class one of the students said, "I have a terrible headache." I thought to myself, "This is not a good way to start off our class. A headache is very distracting and may end up putting the person and others in a negative state and they won't be able to learn. What to do? What to say?" Then I remembered a realization I'd had while I was frustrated by noise one time when I was meditating: "There are no perfect conditions for meditation." When I had this thought, I was able to dive deeply in to meditation. So I shared it with the class.

"Remember, there are no perfect conditions for meditation. Sometimes our body will ache, our head will ache, there will be too much noise and distraction, our mind will not be quiet, our body too fidgety, and then you will get frustrated and stop your practice. When you let go of the ideal or perfect time, space and situation for meditation, meditation will happen. The more you think about how imperfect a situation is, the more you create tension and stress. However, if you remind yourself that there is no perfect condition, you will accept your situation, and as soon as you accept and acknowledge it, the tension will disappear, you will be able to relax, and go deep."

To support my suggestion to them, I shared my experience meditating in Iraq. One day I came back from a convoy and wanted to meditate. Convoys tended to kick up my adrenaline levels because, as I drove the ambulances, I had to worry and keep an eye out for roadside bombs, gunfire, or mortar attacks. Convoys were long. Sometimes I would have to drive three hours one way and three hours back. I always turned to meditation to recenter and reground myself. I was already tired, but I was missing my soul and spending quiet time with myself. When I sat on my bed in cross-legged position, closed my eyes, and took a deep breath in, I was ready to go deeply into my soul. As soon as I started to relax, the soldier next to me decided to blast hip-hop music on their stereo. My mind reacted, "Are you serious? I want to meditate and now there's loud music?" I got angry, frustrated, and upset. I desperately needed to meditate. I then reminded myself, "Hey, forget about what is happening on the outside. Figure out a way to relax despite the loud music." Using my concentration power and becoming aware of my breath, my attention started turning inward again, I started to slowly relax, and I went very deeply into meditation. It was one of the deepest meditation experiences I'd ever had and it lasted over an hour—it was pure joy, peace, and bliss. I needed it.

As a spiritual person, we must realize there is no *perfect*. Once we understand this deeply, our practices and experiences will change. There is no perfect meditation, because it will always change. Our goal should be to always be in the flow, relaxed, and accept whatever comes our way. We meet meditation challenges with acknowledgment and acceptance, and once the mind accepts, the mind cooperates, quiets down, and eventually moves out of the way. When we are free of the *perfect* meditation, we can truly let go and relax.

We should strive to always be able to calm ourselves down, bypass any negative thoughts or emotions, and go deeply into our soul in any moment. We shouldn't have to wait….ever. We need to develop that inner awareness, strength, and good habit to always go beyond. If you give up too quickly, you will miss out on very deep meditation and knowing your soul.

Meditation is an effortless state of consciousness. Meditation is who you are. It is your soul's nature. Always do your best to go beyond the body and mind challenges. Relax more and more, little by little. Never judge your meditation practices.

Meditation is your path to enlightenment. Meditation is the state where you can gain self-realization, deep understanding, right vision, and right knowledge. Meditation burns your karma. Meditation awakens you to your soul. Meditation is what your soul yearns for always.

The more you can be in meditation, the more you will grow. Remember, it's not about minutes, but the quality of that time. Even a few seconds of real meditation are tremendous. As times goes on, it will increase by itself. Meditation is something you cannot force. Meditation is something that happens. Enlightenment cannot be forced, no matter how bad you want it. When you are free of all your karma and 100% in soul, you will attain your enlightenment. Stay on track. Stick to your discipline. Your practice will save you!

Acharya Shree has mentioned these words from the Upanishads:

*Tamaso Ma Jyotir Gamaye.*
*Mrityor Ma Amritam Gamaye.*
*Asato Ma Sad Gamaye.*

*Meditation will always lead you from darkness to light.*
*Meditation will always lead you from death to bliss and ecstasy.*
*Meditation will always lead you from mortality to immortality.*

Activity: Thirty minutes in meditation.

Set aside time today to totally relax for thirty minutes. Before you enter a meditative state, I encourage you to do breathing exercises, mantras, and some yoga before you lay down to totally relax. Remember, when the body is without tension and the mind is calm, you can jump into meditation.

Meditation is your freedom.

# :: WATER FAST ::

Water fasting is one of the fastest ways to burn karma. Like all things that burn karma, it is not that easy. The reason water fasting burns karma quickly is because it creates a fire. Anything that creates heat, such as certain breathing techniques and deep levels of meditation, burns your toxins and karma.

The body is full of toxins and the mind can be filled with poison—negative thoughts, anger, stress, frustration, etc. When the body and mind are filled with pollution, it blocks the soul. The goal of the spiritual path is to burn your karma and remove all those clouds which block your right vision, right knowledge, and right conduct. Water fasting is another

187

practice that you can integrate into your spiritual life.

I will warn you here: water fasting is not for everyone, and each body is different. Most can do a twenty-four-hour water fast except if you are on medications or your doctor advises against it. In general, it is safe to do a twenty-four-hour water fast.

There are many reasons why people water fast: sometimes you have to fast before having surgery or having your blood drawn, some want to lose weight (we do not advise to fast just for weight loss, as proper diet and exercise are required to reduce any kind of weight and maintain that loss of weight), some want to cleanse their body, some want mental clarity, some want to heal their body of certain diseases—like cancer, and some want to burn karma.

Water fasting purifies the body, mind, and soul. The benefits of water fasting include a healthier body, removing toxins and disease, preventative care, removing physical pain, emotional and mental negativities, gaining clarity, eliminating confusion, finding answers within, and burning karma, to name a few. For centuries, fasting has been one of the main spiritual practices to help the soul grow.

Remember, you should only eat to survive, not to enjoy the

taste and luxury of food. Eating (and fulfilling our desires for a full stomach and tasty food) is one of the body's greatest addictions. Anything you indulge in too much brings karma. We don't want more karma, right?

Acharya Shree advises to do at least one twenty-four-hour water fast during the year in order to help reset and reboot the system. The body needs rest from digesting too. All of us at Siddhayatan normally do this at the end of Paryushan. Paryushan is an eight-day celebration that is focused on knowing and awakening the soul. On the eighth day we fast. This spiritual week is usually in August or September. The monks and monks-in-training at Siddhayatan usually fast once a month, sometimes even more.

If you would like to water fast for spiritual purposes, we suggest an extended fast. This could mean three days, seven days, ten days, fourteen days, and even up to thirty days. We have had several guests come for a Water Fasting Retreat at Siddhayatan for over thirty days. Some even went thirty-eight days on water. Like all practices, take baby steps. If you haven't tried it yet, try fasting for just twenty-four hours.

Water fasting is not easy, but it does increase your confidence and willpower. You have been raised to believe that you cannot survive without food. It might even be scary for you to think that you would have to spend twenty-four hours consuming nothing but water. In reality, you can survive. Acharya Shree says certain body types can survive on only water for up to ninety days.

It is important to mention that each body is different regarding fasting. Some can fast for very long periods of time. Some can only fast a few days. Both are okay. However, it is very important not to compare. Whether it is water fasting, your progress on the spiritual path, or anything in life, never compare.

For extended fasts, such as over five days, I highly suggest going to a center and fasting under guidance. This way you can break your fast properly and your body does not get hurt. For extended fasts over ten days, the most critical time is not the time when they are without food, but the time of breaking fast. I want you to be aware of this in case you consider doing a long fast. We provide guidance for water fasts at Siddhayatan.

From personal experience, my body is unable to fast. Even though I would like to do extended fasts to burn as much karma as I can, my body is not able. Acharya Shree says my body-type cannot handle it. My body is really acidic and gets weak easily. For my body, he said I can go up to seven days safely, if I would like to. And seven days would leave me very weak. Though, someone else may not experience that kind of weakness until day twenty-one of their water fast. Because my body is acidic, I actually now prefer to dry fast. That means fasting without food *and* water. This is faster than water-fasting regarding burning karma. Acharya Shree says one can do up to twenty-four hours safely. It's not that easy, but after experience with water fasting, and if you are interested and determined to remove karma, you might consider dry-fasting for twenty-four hours. In some cases, a dry fast can count as two days of water fasting.

Water fasting can help you physically, emotionally, mentally, and most important, spiritually. If you would like to do a water fast, my suggestions are:

~ Don't have a heavy last meal
~ Don't have acidic foods as part of your last meal
~ Try to do only minimal work

It's normal to feel tired, experience headaches, and even some pain. I suggest breaking your twenty-four-hour water fast with light and soft foods such as oatmeal, soup, light beans, mashed potatoes, and fruits.

When you water fast, especially for longer periods, you invite your karma to the surface. You voluntarily go through pain and suffering. (It's not easy to fast.) Sometimes a lot of emotional and mental things will come up from your past, and you will need to face them and go through it. It could be things you never knew happened to you or things you went through but you suppressed and tried to forget about. Fasting will burn that karma, pain, and suffering. It may be difficult to go through, but it is all a good thing. Whatever helps you burn karma is a good thing. Any time you feel that life is painful, remind yourself that you had caused pain and suffering to someone else at some point in your soul's lifetime (previous lives), and now have to take responsibility. You cannot escape karma, but you can reduce and burn it. When you understand these basic laws of karma, life changes.

You ultimately know, understand, and fully realize that whatever you go through in life is a result of good and bad karma—then you do not experience suffering. Maybe you still have to go through some pain, but it doesn't bother you. Suffering comes from attachment, resistance, and lack of right vision and understanding. When your karma is over, all that remains is bliss. When you understand and know the true reality, you are free.

Activity: Water fast for twenty-four hours.

One way to start the fasting experience is to start at 6:00

am and drink water until the following day at 6:00 am. A good day to do the fast is from Saturday morning to Sunday morning, this way you can recover and eat breakfast.

# :: RESPECT YOUR BODY ::

Your human body is the temple of the living God. That living God is your soul. You are God and God is you. Would you let your divine, pure, powerful, and beautiful soul live in a house that is full of grease, leaks, broken drywall and ceilings, cracks all over the place, mold, rodents, and insects everywhere? Of course not. When you respect yourself, respect your soul, and respect your body-temple, you will take care of it. A broken house—a weak or unhealthy body—cannot take your soul to its freedom.

The first way to respect your body and create a strong instrument for your soul to improve itself is having a healthy diet.

Acharya Shree always shares this story with visitors:

All cars need their oil changed, right? If you do not maintain your car by changing its oil, it won't work. It will stop running. And when you go to change the oil, can you put cooking oil in your car? No, of course not. Can you put grease in your car? No, the car wouldn't work. There is a specific oil for cars to use. Without the right oil and fuel, your car will not work. This also applies to your body. You cannot put just anything into your body, otherwise it will become weak, have disease or medical issues, or not last as long as it is meant to. You need to put the right food into your body.

There are many medical physicians and health experts who promote what they believe is right for their body. Sometimes they contradict each other. A lot of doctors and experts focus on protein. Read *The China Study* by T. Colin Campbell. It will open your eyes to the many myths about protein. What is important to remember is that an expert's focus is only on creating a healthy body, they are not thinking about liberating your soul. Most of them do not have the vision to consider what is needed to awaken, transform, and achieve your greatest spiritual goals. You need to have a healthy and *pure* body in order to advance spiritually. Being healthy is not enough. A pure body means it is free of toxins and any meals

196

you had were not a result of violence.

There are three types of food: sattvic, tamasic, and rajasic —light, heavy and very rich. Light food is certain vegetables, fruits, grains, rice, and beans. It will take approximately four to eight hours to digest depending on your metabolic rate. Heavy food takes twice the amount of time and rich food even longer.

The energy required to digest light food is minimal compared to heavier and richer foods. Heavier foods such as pasta, fish, and chicken can take up to twenty-four hours to digest one meal. Richer foods, fried foods, beef, and pork can take up to seventy-two hours to digest one meal.

For example, if you eat one meal containing meat, it will sit in your intestines for three days. Three days is a long time. If you forget to put your leftover meat away and leave it on the kitchen counter it will get rotten and create a lot of bacteria. If you eat it, it can make you sick. Can you imagine all the meat that's sitting in your intestines as of now—it's creating sickness and disease? Some people have meat with every single meal. It's no wonder they end up with high cholesterol, high blood pressure, diabetes, heart problems, and much more. Respect your body. Eat light foods so you free up energy that is being used for digestion and use it instead towards your meditation

197

and spiritual practices.

If you are not vegetarian, a light diet may not sound appealing—rice, beans, grains, vegetables, and fruits? Maybe in your mind it is a plate of steamed vegetables and you would have to eat that for the rest of your life. No. Don't let your mind fool you. You can eat tasty light foods too. Guests at Siddhayatan are surprised when we serve them delicious meals that are healthy and light. They were expecting plain vegetables.

Remember, too, your goal is to liberate yourself from strong desires that enhance any of your senses. If you are too much into eating and taste, practice *mini-fasting*. This means eat a little less than what you would normally eat. It automatically helps you regain control. Or, you can always skip a meal. That is also another form of fasting. You want to be a master of yourself, don't let food take you away from your self-mastery. Acharya Shree says the desire for tasty and filling food is one of the greatest addictions and habits to break. Free your soul of any desires, especially food desires. Care for your body.

Another way to respect your body is not to put any alcohol, smoke, or drugs into it. One female army veteran came for the "Break Free of Addiction Retreat." She was drinking and smoking a lot. Her main goal was to stop drinking. I remember telling her that in order to break any addiction, you should have a strong reason and purpose behind it, otherwise it is easy to fall back into it. She asked if I had smoked or drank before. I said yes. I used to smoke a lot and was addicted. I started smoking at age thirteen. I quit a few times, but it never lasted. I quit smoking about a month and half after returning from war. I told myself no more, as one night I drank and smoked too much and was sick during the evening. My first taste of alcohol was at age fifteen, and I would drink often with friends. When I was in the military, both became a stronger addiction. She asked how I was able to quit. I told her, firstly, "Acharya Shree taught me breathing techniques and Purnam Yoga to help me." Secondly, "One of the last times I drank, I attended a lecture at the ashram on a hangover." Thirdly, "I didn't follow through on one of my appointments with Acharya Shree because I was sick as a result of drinking." Lastly, "The last time I drank, I was so angry I almost drove down a huge snowy mountain drunk, and could have died."

My drinking increased because of war. It hit me hard, the final night I drank, what I was really doing to myself. I was conflicted. I wanted to be spiritual. I wanted to be free. And there I was crying at the wheel, angry and helpless, and nearly committing suicide. I promised myself no more. I knew I wanted to be a monk and I needed to stop drinking. I knew I wanted to find myself. I was tired of feeling lost. War had changed me. It made me feel disconnected. Through understanding and practice it dropped by itself. I never looked back. April 9, 2006, was the last time I drank and said good-bye to alcohol.

I told her, when you have a strong reason, especially a spiritual reason, you will drop the addiction. The click will happen. You won't have to fear returning to it either. I was free. You can be free too.

For my own path, I knew I had to give up three things: meat, smoking, and drinking. I gave up all three in 2006. My reason was rooted in spiritual advancement.

Always watch what you put in to your body. Too much of anything is not good for you. Too much sugar, too much dairy, too much salt, too many chilies, too many fried foods, too much caffeine, is not good for the body and can create imbalance. Imbalance can lead to your body getting sick and feeling tired, having scattered energy, and experiencing negative thoughts, nightmares, headaches, and difficulty sleeping.

It is best not to eat or drink anything too late in the evening. The reason is your third chakra is closed and doesn't have much energy to digest your food. Acharya Shree suggests eating three hours before you plan to sleep. It is also not a good idea to have midnight snacks. It disturbs your body, mind, and sleep. Control your senses. Be healthy.

ACTIVITY: Reflect and write.

How have you been disrespectful to your body and what habits can you start changing?

When you respect your body, it means you are respecting the temple of the living God, you. The real you. Go beyond the clouds that cover your soul. Start removing the pollution that currently lives in your body and free yourself of all those toxins. If you cannot improve all aspects right now, that is okay, at least start becoming more aware. Begin to minimize what you can and one day, as a result of your effort, many of your desires will disappear.

# :: LIFE PURPOSE ::

I used to hide under the table a lot. I would lie across the chairs so that if anyone looked under the table, they would not find me. I did this when I was six to seven years old. It was during this time I first began experiencing my soul. I used to enter the dark space for four to six hours. I didn't know until much later, when Acharya Shree told me, I was actually in high states of meditation. In my child-mind I knew whatever I was doing felt good, that there was some kind of infinite power in it—I could feel it—and I wanted to know and taste more of it. I would always ask, "Who am I? Who is God? What is death? What is the purpose of my life?"

One evening, I was in my grandma's room where I slept.

She was traveling and I was completely alone in her room. As I lay there resting on the bed at eight pm, I first started to stare at the ceiling with the help of my little night light. I had started my rounds of deep thinking—Who am I? Really, who am I? What is the purpose of my life? What is it that I need to discover? As I lay there thinking, I eventually rolled over, my forehead resting on my arms, face to the pillow. That was my way (practice) of going deep back them. Somehow it helped me to focus and to stay away from distraction. All of a sudden I jumped into the dark space. I began to see swirls of purple and black light. On this particular evening, I wanted to go deeper than I normally did. Suddenly I was out of my body. I was scared, yet trusted the experience. My soul went to the ocean first, which was uplifting and made me happy, and then I came back to my city. I saw the rooftops of many buildings and homes. On several occasions I entered homes and observed what was happening. I began to feel very sad and full of pain. I saw children getting physically and sexually abused. Outside a drug store I saw a homeless man who was very depressed. I saw women getting beaten by their husbands. I saw drug users and alcoholics. My little soul was full of pain. Somehow, my soul was able to tune in and feel all the pain they were feeling. I tried to help some of them, but I couldn't. They couldn't see me. They were each crying in their own way. As I continued to fly around the city, the overwhelming and enormous pain intensified. As a six-year-old, I didn't know what pain really was, until that experience. After I came back into my body, I was still immersed in the dark space. I was quiet, still, and in deep meditation. My soul said to me, "Your purpose in life is to help people remove their pain." My mind began to flood with thoughts of how I would do that. One day, I will write books. One day, I will speak. One day, I will write a film. I want to make people laugh, so at least for a moment their pain is relieved. My little heart was completely broken. I thought the world was good. But inside homes and workplaces, I saw with my own soul-eyes that people have so much pain inside. They experience so much. They carry it around and tell no one. They were really good actors — smiling on the outside, suffering on the inside. I was especially connected to teenagers. I saw that they were abused, but never said anything to anyone — they were struggling to make sense of their lives, trying to find an identity, yet holding on to their deep secrets of abuse. My purpose was first revealed to me when I was six years old. I was reminded of my purpose when I was twelve years old and attended my first Catholic spiritual retreat at school for the youth of the parish. I knew I was supposed to serve the community. Then when I was eighteen years old, and after I had begun my spiritual journey, I was writing and had asked myself the question: "What is the purpose of my life?" I began writing and didn't even know what I was writing. I was in a state of meditation. I wasn't in my mind. Once I was done writing, I turned the paper over, and put my forehead on my arms, like the night when I'd had my first spiritual awakening. I saw only black, I felt the space. I asked myself, "Did I write the truth? Did my mind enter? Did my ego enter?" I wrote the truth. Now I had to flip it over and read my reality.

"The purpose of your life is to be a nun and help others spiritually. You will wear white one day. You understand pain and you will help others remove that pain."

I knew I didn't want to be a Catholic nun. I knew I didn't want to be part of any religion. I didn't know how I would end up being a spiritual teacher and how I would start wearing white, but I knew that because it was truth, it would happen. I didn't know how, only that it would. Two years later I met Acharya Shree, when I was twenty. He told me that one day I would get initiated and even liberated, but that I needed his guidance to help me get there.

I told him, "I have big work to do. I know I have a big purpose. I want to help a lot of people." "You will," he said. "But first you need to light yourself. How do you expect to light other candles if you yourself are not lit? First light yourself, then you can go and light the world."

Since I was young, I always knew my purpose: It was to help people. I wanted to help people be free of their pain and suffering. I experienced pain and suffering in my own life—losing my mom, feeling unloved and uncared for by my dad, going to war, lots of inner conflict, and so much more. I experienced a lot, as you have in your own way. I'm grateful for all of it, because I truly understand what pain is and how to be free from it.

The reason I have shared such an intimate story with you is because you also have a purpose, and you need to make it come to life.

The question is, have you figured it out?

People come for retreat because they want to find their purpose. They are tired of living by what everyone else wants and are finally ready to do what their heart really wants to do. You want to live by your own dreams, your own vision, and your own ideas. And you should!

Don't let anyone stop you. Not even your biggest enemy, yourself.

Most people have a dream to somehow help people. It stems from a motivation of either experiencing pain, seeing someone else in pain, or being inspired by a story or person because their heart was touched. You want to make a difference.

I encourage you to change the world. We need a better world. We need a world filled with souls who live by heart and not by mind. We need a world filled with compassion and tolerance, not hate, judgment, and ego.

Hope for a better world starts with YOU.

What is the purpose of your life? What in the world are you tired of seeing? Why? Why does it bother you? What are you going to do about it? Do you think you can live your entire life not doing anything about it? Do you want to have a meaningful life?

Then do something.

Take action.

When you do anything with your heart and soul, it doesn't feel like work. When your passion and the reason behind the things you do takes over, nothing will stop you, no matter the small or big challenges. You know you will overcome them somehow. You will do everything and anything to fulfill your purpose.

Shine Through Wisdom

When you follow your heart, do what you truly want to do, in combination with spirituality, you will make a huge difference. As you improve yourself and grow spiritually, you will gain the right vision and right knowledge to help you in your purpose and your endeavors to fulfill that purpose. Thus, your impact is even greater.

Keep working on yourself. Figure out your purpose in life, then live with that purpose always lit in your heart. When you live a meaningful life, as defined by you, you will truly be happy. You will feel complete. You will be soaring.

Activity: Reflect and write.

In your journal, write the purpose of your life.

Ask yourself why it means so much to you. What inspired your purpose? Then describe how you would feel if you didn't fulfill that purpose and write down ways or steps you can take to begin fulfilling that purpose.

Don't feel like you have a purpose? Then create one for yourself. :)

When you live with purpose, when you live with soul, your life will take a stunning twist.

# :: BEYOND PROBLEMS ::

Problems can bring uncertainty, difficulty, and even pain into your life. They can cause you stress, anxiety, worry, heartache, anger, and make you over think. At the same time, problems make you stronger—that is for the spiritual practitioner.

When you are a spiritual person, you view life completely differently from others. You take responsibility for your life. You are responsible for how you think, feel, speak, and act. You understand there is a deep reason why things happen in life; karma—sometimes you like it, sometimes you don't. As a spiritual practitioner, you believe and trust in yourself that you will figure out a solution. If one is not a spiritual practitioner, or more on the superficial side of spirituality, they will play the complain and blame game. "Why God, why are you doing this to me?" Or, "It's not fair." "Life is too hard, my problems are overwhelming, I can't take this anymore," and then they are full of frustration. The difference between you and them is that you begin to see your problems as a positive, and not as a negative.

No one really likes problems. However, it's the challenges that make you stronger. Unless you test yourself, you can never know your own inner strength, courage, bravery, and fearlessness.

According to Acharya Shree, humans cannot be without problems. The reason is because they always live in the mind. The mind doesn't like stillness, it doesn't like to be quiet, so it needs to create problems. If you do not give the mind something to do, it can go crazy. That's why it is important to always be focused and productive. A bored mind is never a good thing. War happens because of problems. If there are no problems, the mind will create problems. The untamed mind is a dangerous thing. That's why the mind can be a blessing and a curse. It is a curse as it creates problems and sucks you into them. Yet, the mind can be a blessing because it becomes an instrument to your soul, so you can focus on practices and enter the depths of your soul.

Shine Through Wisdom

When you are free of mind, you are liberated.

There are many ways to help free your mind as given throughout the book. Awareness, focus, changing mental habits, breathing techniques, mantras, and much more. These teachings and techniques help you free your mind and free your soul.

What also helps you become free is facing your problems. Taking responsibility. Not escaping, but rather facing them. I know some spiritual people who wish they could "run to the forest and live in a hut." These are escapers. Even if they are in the jungle, they have not mastered their mind, and will always be a slave to the mind. Constantly bothered. No peace. When you face your problems, when you face all the negative things the mind creates, you become stronger. Or as Acharya Shree says for the spiritual practitioner, "Problems make you shine even more."

He once shared an example that has stuck with me.

"To make gold shine, you can put some polish on it and make it a little nice. Or, you can throw it in the fire. When you put gold in the fire it will shine so brightly. A spiritual practitioner is like the gold in the fire. Yes, things might be a little painful at first, but you withstand the heat, you face your

213

challenges and problems, and then you emerge from your problems, pain, and suffering by shining. Don't be afraid of problems. Jump in and face it."

The soul will continue to be far away from you if you do not face your problems. A spiritual practitioner welcomes problems, because it is a chance to shine and grow—you force yourself to grow, you force yourself to go through the pain and challenges, because you know in the end you will be free. The more you run away or escape, suppress your problems, pretend they don't exist, or that "the universe will take care of it," you will never be free. As the common saying goes, "No pain, no gain."

Believe and trust in yourself that you can get through any problems. I've survived my mom's death, war, my own self-hate, and much more. I never thought that would've been possible, but have since realized how much strength I had. Now I know you've experienced your share of pain and suffering too. You know what? You are still alive, you are breathing, and you have a new spiritual foundation that will help you face anything that comes your way. Remember, the more you work on yourself, the more clarity comes. With clarity, you get solutions to your problems, not temporary answers. For problems there can be many answers, however, as a spiritual person you are not satisfied with answers. You

214

seek solutions.

Spirituality is your solution. Continue working hard on yourself. Deepen your understanding about life and soul. When you have right vision, right knowledge, and right conduct you will be free. You will free of problems, karma, and mind. You will be liberated.

Activity: Reflect and write.

What problems overwhelm you? Is there anything you can do it about it? If not, why are you still holding on to it and worrying about it and being affected by it? If it's not in your hands, flow. You will figure out a solution. When you relax, solutions come.

# :: HUMBLENESS ::

The ego is a major cloud of pollution that covers the soul. It is very subtle, yet dominates and influences our lives—the way we think, feel, and act. In ego mode, we can be stubborn, resistant, always comparing ourselves to others, angry, depressed, sad and feeling inferior. There are many types of ego, however, we'll focus on the main eight:

**Knowledge-Ego.** When someone is full of knowledge-ego, they can be arrogant and prideful about all the things they know. Their knowledge can span from a variety of topics— science, spirituality, sports, scriptures, religion, economics, politics, construction, etc. Those with knowledge-ego have convinced themselves that they are better or superior because

217

of their knowledge. Their self-esteem and self-concept are based on their knowledge. They can appear as show-offs, thus turning people off.

**Respect-Ego.** When someone is full of respect-ego, it means they desire to be worshipped, recognized, honored, famous, appreciated, glorified, thought highly of, or need to be right, or really love power—to name a few. When they are disrespected, they can become negative, angry or hurt. The respect-ego is also a type of superiority and arrogance.

**Social Class-Ego.** Even though it doesn't seem like it, the class system still permeates society. There is the lower class, middle class, upper class, and the elite, along with many other forms of class. When someone is in class-ego, they believe they are better than everyone because of the class to which they belong. Some are very proud that they are born into a rich or royal family. For example, one can be proud to be born into the samurai class or Brahmin class.

**Race-Ego.** When someone has race-ego, they are very proud to be from a certain culture or race. They think by being white, black, red, yellow or any other skin-tone color they are better than everyone. Racism will continue to hurt our world and create wars because of race-ego. No country is best. No race is best. No religion is best. No gender is best. No orientation is best. We need to get away from this "we're the best" culture. You be the best you can be. That is the best thing.

**Competitive-Ego.** When someone has a competitive-ego, they always strive to be the best, number one. They cannot accept loss as an option, and they always have to win. They have the mindset, "No one can compete with me. I'm too good." They can go to the extreme to hurt others or make others feel bad about themselves in order to achieve "best status."

**Rich-Ego.** When someone thinks they are better and superior to everyone because of their wealth and riches. Wealth can take many forms: a lot of money in the bank, a lot of clothes, a lot of shoes, or jewelry. No one likes or appreciates those who are arrogant about money and wealth.

**Sadhana-Ego.** When someone believes they are better than everyone because of their spiritual practices. For example, one might boast that they can meditate long hours, water fast for many days, do tratka for 3 hours without blinking, hold a yoga posture for a very long time, or they might believe they are better for being "spiritual" compared to those who are "non-spiritual."

**Beauty-Ego.** When someone has beauty-ego they are really into their looks and believe they are better looking than others. They take pride in their looks—whether it is their face, body or any other feature. Their beauty goes to their head and cause them to be arrogant. They might think, "I'm way prettier than you." Or, "Wow, I look so good," as they look in the mirror.

The 8 types of ego described above give you a general idea of the different types of ego. I described the superior, prideful or arrogant aspect of them. Ego is not limited to the superior aspect, but also the inferior—the ego can get very hurt, too.

When the ego is hurt or feels inferior one might feel that they are not smart or good enough, are shy or a loser, don't have a sharp memory, are undeserving or never appreciated, hurt, not good looking enough, may wish they were born as another race or into another family, might feel bad they are poor or in a middle-class family, continuously live in fear, afraid of being noticed, don't believe in themselves, etc. Where there is superiority in the mind, there is also inferiority. Where there is ego, soul is not present. When there is no ego, only soul remains.

It's important to live in a balanced way. To always flow. When you are balanced and in the flow, you will be unaffected by the ego and mind and all the ups and downs in life. If you receive praise, you don't get an ego about it. If you receive criticism, your ego doesn't hurt.

One day, I asked Acharya Shree how to overcome my fears of humiliation, rejection, and caring about what people think. I was tired of living in fear. How could I change the world if I was afraid of it? I wanted to live courageously and boldly. I didn't want to continue living in my chains. He told me, "You need to flow. You need to adjust. Whether you like or dislike it when the weather is cold, it will be cold. If you don't like it, you have to accept it. You cannot change anything about it. You must adjust to it. When people throw stones at you and criticize you, accept it, don't resist it and adjust. Keep flowing. Keep moving on. Don't let anyone or even yourself stop you."

It became clear—when you flow, ego goes.

The way to begin dissolving or crushing your ego is to practice humbleness. When you are humble, you stay down-to-earth. When you are in ego, you are high up in the sky, and when you fall from the sky, it hurts. It's best to stay low. You are neither better nor less than anyone.

One way to practice humbleness is to say, "I'm sorry." It's

difficult for those who live in ego to say these two words, but they are the most powerful. They can unite family, friends, coworkers, and loved ones. "I'm sorry" can remove all the tension and resistance. It can let things flow again.

Acharya Shree suggests to be sweet. Be sweet with your words. When you are sweet in your words and deeds, most if not everyone will be your friend. If you are always kind and nice, who can be mean or put down a sweet person? A genuine sweetness can be your nature. As the saying goes, "kill them with kindness." (Nonviolently, of course!)

One thing I would like to clarify is self-pride vs. ego. I strongly believe we should be proud of ourselves. We should feel that we are good enough, smart, beautiful, strong, equal, and deserving of all the greatness and happiness that life has to offer. We respect ourselves. This kind of pride comes from a deep understanding, loving, and acceptance of who we are. There is no superiority or inferiority in self-pride. Ego is pride, but it is a pride that takes you away from soul. Self-pride brings you to soul.

Activity: Reflect and write.

Identify which types of ego you have and how you will help reduce them.

Awareness is like the piercing light which destroys all darkness. As you grow on the spiritual path, and as your awareness develops, you will begin to witness when the mind and ego try to influence you. In those moments, you will be able to humble yourself quickly and switch your thinking. Or, when the time and situation calls for it, say, "I'm sorry."

Be sweet, my friends. Be kind. Be loving.

We always admire people who are down to earth, "real", and humble. Be one of them.

# :: KARMA ::

In order to free your soul, you must know about karma. You need to understand how it is collected, how it affects your life, and most important, how to remove it. This book has been dedicated to show you how to remove it—from teachings, techniques, and all the tips shared. I've referred to karma as pollution, clouds, dirt, dust, and particles throughout the book, but now it's time to understand it fully.

Karma is a universal law, which states that you collect karmic particles based on your intention combined with your actions—whether mental, emotional, physical, or by speech. It's a common saying, "Do good, get good karma. Do bad, get bad karma," but karma is often misunderstood. There is a

225

depth to karma that many are not aware of. The science and details, such as how the soul collects karmic particles, the workings of the eight *ghatiya* and *aghatiya* categories of karma, what practices can be used to dissolve specific karmas, and the states of consciousness that the soul rises through towards enlightenment and liberation, are some examples of the intricacies of karma that only a master can help you to understand. Acharya Shree has helped me and so I pass it on to you.

In each moment, whether sleeping or awake, karma is being accumulated as a result of open holes — spiritual ignorance — where karmic particles pour in and mix together with your soul. For example, if you have not conquered your anger 100%, anger will continue to be a source for you to collect karma. Or, if you have not dissolved your jealousy 100%, you will be able to collect karma when you are jealous. It is easy to dismiss the possibility of having these karmas if you don't experience something negative like anger, but the particles that disturb the soul are subtle, so it is difficult to know when they are active on the surface. Often times, these subtleties come from karma collected in previous lives, therefore you may not be aware of how they are affecting your spirituality in this life. Unless you work on yourself and practice awareness, you will always collect karma. The more karma you collect, the less opportunities the soul has to awaken itself and break through the clouds.

It is because of karma that the cycle of birth and death continues. When the time comes—after much effort and deep understanding—the soul will be free, realize its enlightenment, and become liberated from the cycle at the end of that life.

To be free, we need to stop collecting new karma by closing the open sources (like plugging the in-flow of water into a reservoir), then dispose of the karma we've already collected throughout our countless lifetimes (draining what's left within the reservoir). Even if you dissolve just a tiny bit of karma, it is a great weight lifted off your soul.

Karma can be broken down into eight categories. Four are called *ghatiya*, which are the karmas that obstruct the soul from knowing itself. The other four are called *aghatiya*, which are about the body where the soul dwells: how long the body can survive *(ayu karma)*; the type of body like bacteria, insect, animal, or human body *(nam karma)*; societal status, such as being born in a poor or wealthy family *(gotra karma)*; and lastly, the mental, emotional, and physical pain and suffering experienced *(vedaniya karma)*. Because you are on the spiritual path, it is very important to understand the karma categories and the ways they block your soul. When you understand karma, you will know how to free yourself.

## THE FOUR GHATIYA CATEGORIES

*Jñānāvaraṇīya Karma*. These karmas obscure the soul from its own knowledge.

*1. Mati-Jñānāvaraṇīya Karma* blocks the knowledge transmitted to the senses. (i.e. when you read something and forget what you have read, or if you put your hand in boiling water and you feel it is cold.)

*2. Sruta-Jñānāvaraṇīya Karma* blocks the knowledge acquired by interpretation. (i.e. when you are listening to a teacher, the concept is not easily grasped, or you fall asleep or misinterpret words, symbols, and gestures.)

*3. Avadhi-Jñānāvaraṇīya Karma* blocks knowledge in a limited way. (i.e. your inner-vision is blocked from experiencing or describing objects up to a certain distance from where you are located.)

*4. Manah-Jñānāvaraṇīya Karma* blocks you from seeing mind-particles. (i.e. you cannot see if your mind or another's mind is playing games or tricks on you.)

*5. Kevala-Jñānāvaraṇīya Karma* blocks absolute knowing of the soul. (i.e. when you are on the wrong path, or not seeking spirituality, you are unable to have soul-knowing.)

*Darśanāvaraṇīya Karma.* These karmas block the soul

from having right vision, or seeing things as they really are.

*1. Chaksur-Darśanāvaranīya Karma* blocks visual perception. (i.e. you cannot see with your eyes, are born blind, color-blind, etc.)

*2. Cchaksur-Darśanāvaranīya Karma* blocks all the other senses, except your eyes. (i.e. you are not able to hear, smell, taste, feel.)

*3. Avadhi-Darśanāvaranīya Karma* creates limited vision. (i.e. a person might express their spirituality using unfamiliar language and you immediately judge and dismiss them as non-spiritual. You are not seeing them as they really are — spiritual, but disguised.)

*4. Kevala-Darśanāvaranīya Karma* blocks your clear vision of the soul. (i.e. you do not have any glimpses from the soul or cannot see through to the soul.)

***Mohanīya Karma.*** These karmas create delusion around the soul about what is truth and how to act. It is considered the most dangerous and most difficult to dissolve, because these are the largest and easiest holes to fall through, which will bring you a lot of karma.

*1. Darśana-Mohanīya Karma* hinders understanding of spirituality and truth.

*2. Mithyātva-Karma* causes beliefs in false teachings and

false gurus and prophets. (i.e. a person gets trapped into fake spiritual teachings and sees false gurus as saints.)

3. *Cāritra-Mohanīya Karma* disturbs right conduct and is mostly produced by the four passions *(kṣhāyaṣ)*: anger *(krodha,* ego *(māna)*, deceitfulness *(māyā)*, and greed *(lobha)*. Karma is also collected through six non-passions *(nokṣhāyaṣ)*: evil laughing *(hāṣaya)*, liking *(rati)*, disliking *(arati)*, sorrow *(ṣoka)*, fear *(bhaya)*, and disgust *(jugupṣā)*. In addition, karma is collected in desiring and lusting for sexual pleasures *(vedaṣ)* with a man, woman, or hermaphrodite—this excludes expressing love.

***Antarāya Karma.*** These karmas block the soul from enjoyment and achievement.

*1. Dāna-Antarāya Karma* prevents you from achieving any kind of success. It is collected when you block a person from helping another. (i.e. when you convince someone not to donate to a charity that they are passionate about, then you collect Dāna-Antarāya Karma. As a result of collecting this type of karma, when the time comes that you want to do good and/or achieve any kind of success, something prevents it from happening, and you cry over it and wonder, "Why?")

*2. Lābha-Antarāya Karma* blocks any benefits that could be received throughout your life. (i.e. you distract someone from achieving their goals, so when you should receive the benefit of something good, it is blocked.)

3. *Vīrya-Antarāya Karma* blocks the soul's willpower and physical/mental strength. (i.e. you make a person weak, hurt their self-esteem, or prevent someone from starting the spiritual path, so as a result, you will not have any willpower to achieve your own goals—societal or spiritual.)

The science of karmic law is huge. I mention all of this because it is important to understand why things have happened to you and why you have ups and downs on the spiritual path. Unless you understand karma and its different types, it will be difficult to progress. Often times we blame God, curse others, and are upset when things in life do not go our way. The best thing to do, Acharya Shree says, is to take responsibility and put forth effort to awaken your soul.

I know this is a lot to take in, but it is very important to understand karma, because now you can use the rest of your life as a spiritual practitioner dedicated to removing your karma. All effort counts. Nothing is wasted. Even if it may appear you are getting nowhere at times, you are still changing and transforming. You may not see it, but others will. A master will notice your growth right away.

Activity: Study these different types of karma.

Begin to identify how the above karmas have positively or negatively affected your life. After, decide which spiritual practices you would like in order to start reducing such karma. For example, you can consider water fasting for twenty-four hours to help remove your darśanāvaraṇīya karma, this way you begin to realize and see the Truth with crystal clarity.

# :: SPIRITUAL PRACTICES ::

Inspiration is what gets you started on your spiritual journey; practice is what keeps you on the path. Discipline, dedication, patience and persistence are the backbone of staying on the spiritual track.

Life gets in the way. There are a lot of responsibilities that you have. Many people fall off; they are excited in the beginning, but it slowly fades away. It's a reality, however, don't let that be *your* reality. If you've come this far in your reading, I know you want, deep down, to integrate spirituality into your life. You get it. You've maybe experienced a few clicks, glimpses, and realizations. You don't want to lose. You're committed. Creating a spiritual practice and sticking to

233

it will help you continue to grow and advance in the spiritual life.

You've learned many teachings, techniques, tips, tools, and practices that are helping you become more spiritual day by day. Some stand out more than others, some things you might disagree with, some may seem too "out there," or everything feels right to you.

Since you are nearly at the end of this book, it doesn't mean your spiritual journey and guidance ends. Everything on the path requires effort on your part. So now it's your turn.

My question to you is:

What will be your sadhana for the next thirty-one days?

Creating a set of spiritual practices will help you stay focused on your journey. Consider integrating different techniques daily. Maybe one day you can do breathing techniques, a few mantras, followed by meditation. Maybe another day you can sit for thirty minutes reciting mantras. On another day you can take a vow not to say any abusive words. Maybe once in a while you can do a water fast. Your spiritual practices are totally up to you. Everything helps.

Shine Through Wisdom

To give you a sample set of spiritual practices, you can do the following:

**Day 1.** Deep breathing, two hundred times Kapalbhati, Aum Namo Siddhaanam one hundred and eight times, and sit quietly in meditation for five minutes.

**Day 2.** Deep breathing, three hundred times Kapalbhati, recite all seven chakra activations sounds, twenty-seven times each, followed by five minutes of meditation.

**Day 3.** Do the Sun Salutation three times, followed by two minutes of deep breathing. Then recite Aum Hrim Shrim Klim Arhum Hamsa one hundred and eight times. Sit quietly for fifteen minutes.

**Day 4.** Recite or mentally repeat one mala of the Namokar mantra (first five lines).

**Day 5.** Eat only vegetarian meals. Minimize all violence today. Four hundred Kapalbhati breathing repetitions.

**Day 6.** Spend three minutes doing deep breathing. Then practice Tratka. Do two hundred Kapalbhati breathing repetitions. Recite mentally Aum Namo Siddhaanam one hundred and eight times. Sit for ten minutes of meditation.

**Day 7.** Do most practices mentioned in this book.

Sun Salutation. Deep breathing. Kapalbhati. All mantras. All chakra sounds. Tratka. Meditation for five minutes. And read one chapter from this book at random, for fun.

When I first started learning about spirituality, I wanted to learn and practice everything. I wanted to be super spiritual. I didn't want to waste a single moment, a single opportunity, or miss out on any technique. I went extreme with my spirituality. As a heads up, I want you to avoid being extreme in your practices.

For several months early in my path, I was doing so many techniques, so many practices, and reading so many books because I was excited and determined. I wanted enlightenment right away. I wanted liberation, yesterday. I did too much, too fast, and I actually became adverse to it. Anything you do too much of, you get turned off. When I first met Acharya Shree, I was at a point where I was adverse to spiritual practices for three months. I was in "whatever" mode and didn't care. I knew I wanted to be spiritual, but my body and even mind didn't want to even think about spirituality.

During my first encounter with Acharya Shree, he told me, "Slow and steady wins the race. When you do anything too fast or too extreme, you will fall off the path. It's better to go step-by-step. When you are steady on the path, you will not fall. I am here to guide you."

Anything done in extreme-mode will not last. Maybe you are determined, maybe you are disciplined, but do your practices in a relaxed way. When you are tense about your practices, you are creating stress in your practices—that isn't a peaceful and liberating feeling. Practice in a balanced and disciplined way, and not in a forced way.

It took some time to get back into my practices. I started off with only a few minutes of meditation and then my time for spiritual practices increased over time. Remember, spiritual practices are what save your path and keep you on track. They help reduce your karma. As a result you gain more clarity, transform, release all lower qualities, let go of the past, and most important, connect to your soul.

Activity: Create a spiritual practice.

Go through the book and pick and choose which practices you would like to do. Get a monthly calendar, write those practices on the calendar, and each day, mark an "x" when you complete your sadhana. You can do as little or as much as you'd like, based on your time or inspiration. Key thing is: do something. You will feel accomplished and proud of yourself for making an effort, staying disciplined, and most important, growing.

As Acharya Shree says, "Spirituality is practicality." Do your spiritual practices. I promise you will grow as a result. The more you do it, consistently and over a longer period of time, the more you may feel like a different person. You may finally feel like and be the real you. It's your time.

# :: SPIRITUAL VOWS ::

A spiritual vow is a promise to yourself. When you make such a vow, it symbolizes that you are serious, committed, and dedicated to improving your self and moving forward on your journey. Vows solidify your intention. You might want to grow spiritually and might dedicate some time to practices, however, a vow, a sacred promise to yourself, helps make it concrete.

Is it required? No. But it is helpful and symbolic. Any time you make a vow, it becomes a daily reminder for you to get back on track, get out of your mind, get out of your negativity, overcome laziness, and help you stay committed to breaking through your karma.

A vow is about you and it is for you. Only you benefit from it. It might seem scary to even consider making a vow, a promise, because you might fear it is "too much" or "you are not ready" or it seems "too serious." Your spiritual path is about you—are you not ready to know your true self; don't you take your soul seriously; is spirituality too much for you?

A vow can be for anything, for any length of time. A vow can be, "I promise not to be angry for twenty-four hours." And no matter what, you do your best not to be angry for those twenty-four hours. Or, you can take a vow to water fast for twenty-four hours, and no matter what, you will abstain from food. Or, you can take a lifelong vow to be vegetarian. Or, take a vow to be non-violent. Or, take a vow to never hit someone. When you make any vow, you automatically are minimizing the violence, you create self-awareness, you help close the open sources that bring you karma, and it helps you stay on your journey.

A vow should always come from the heart. It is never forced. Anything forced on the path isn't real.

I remember when I was a young monk, I asked Acharya Shree why he hadn't given me any big rules or particular sadhana to follow daily. In general, he left everything up to me to decide my own practice. In my early days, I was comparing myself to other monks in traditional religions. Their teachers would give them certain practices to do, and they HAD to do them. I was expecting something similar from Acharya Shree. When I became a monk, I figured I needed to meditate at least three hours a day, do one hour of mantras, yoga daily, and much more. Acharya Shree's reply to my question was very powerful and moving, he said, "Why should I give you sadhana to do? Why should I force you to do your practices? When your spiritual practices come from your heart that is what counts. How does feeling punished sound like spirituality to you? I want you to be free. You know what practices are available to you. When you do them wholeheartedly, by your own free will, then you are free. It doesn't make sense for me to tell you what to do, and then you do it, but as you practice you are angry or feel like you're being punished. No. I will not block your freedom."

I've always appreciated Acharya Shree's nontraditional ways. I broke my idea of forced-upon sadhana that day. All things spiritual must come by heart and not force. I voluntarily took vows to lead a nonviolent life and become a monk. I chose monkhood for myself and it has since helped me stay on track and advance tremendously spiritually. I've never looked back. My vows are the world to me. It's my word. It's my word to myself. I cannot turn my back on myself. I've made the commitment. It seems the vow is a part of me and not separate from me. My soul wanted it and now it lives the life it sought.

I bring up the topic of vows because you might feel you want to take your spirituality to the next level and commit now or sometime one day.

To create a vow, you decide on a promise you would like to make to yourself. It could be anything for any length of time. A vow symbolizes your commitment and desire to solidify your path. All you have to do is make a decision, and say out loud "I vow to _____ no matter what."

Remember, when you make an unintentional mistake, it doesn't mean your vow is broken. Practice your awareness and get back on track. It's okay!

Another way to take spiritual vows is by coming to Siddhayatan and meeting Acharya Shree. If he's unavailable, I can give you a spiritual vow. During that time you can let us know what vow you would like to take, we will then repeat the vows in Sanskrit, and at the end you say "Appaanam Vosirami," which translates to "I promise."

Sometimes you may want to take a vow, but do not know which ones to take. As I mentioned before, Acharya Shree mentioned a true spiritual practitioner commits to the following: leads a life of nonviolence (including vegetarianism), does not tell big lies, does not steal, does not take drugs or drink alcohol, does not hunt, does not gamble, does not eat meat, and does not get involved in prostitution (by choice). Many have taken all of these vows, some take a few, and some take different ones. Everything counts. Everything helps. All vows matter.

Acharya Shree gives spiritual names to practitioners who are ready. Usually, they have taken all seven vows, or are working on themselves in order to take up the seven vows. He gives a Sanskrit spiritual name based on their soul's potential. The spiritual name also serves as a reminder to always be on the path. The vows and the spiritual name are for you and your journey. It is something to consider, but I wanted to let you know that you have those options available. Is it necessary? No. Is it helpful? Absolutely.

Activity: Take a vow.

What vow can you take for the next twenty-four hours? Recite out loud: "For the next twenty-four hours I will _____ no matter what."

When you are dedicated to the spiritual path, your whole body, mind, and soul are in it fully. A vow reminds you of your

243

dedication and devotion to your path. A vow reminds you to always be active in your soul. When you are with soul, you are free.

# :: IT'S YOUR TIME ::

Spirituality is the path and process of self-improvement in order to awaken the soul. It is an exciting journey full of challenges and discoveries which lead you to the treasures hidden within you. In this book you have been given teachings, techniques, and tools in order to help you on your path to enlightenment and liberation. As you slowly remove the clouds of ignorance and karmic pollution, you will begin to find and know your true self more and more each day. Now that you have a toolbox full of tools, it's your turn to put them to use and build yourself a strong spiritual foundation. Doing nothing gets you nowhere. Doing a little something, gets you somewhere.

There are five factors that influence each and every moment. The factors are nature, timing, destiny, karma, and effort. Nature can affect your life mostly through weather and natural disasters; timing can affect your life in the sense that the spiritual timing is right for your soul (sometimes it is not the right time to discover certain things, when the timing is right, things begin to happen); destiny is like fate, that certain things are supposed to happen in your life as a result of good and bad karma (you might have the destiny to have a certain profession or do specific global work); karma affects you all the time, but sometimes specific karma comes on the surface and is very strong, it is difficult to escape it, whether it is good or bad karma; and then there is effort. Effort mean you put effort to improve yourself and grow spiritually. Out of the five, you only have control over one of them. And this factor is the most important. What is it? Effort. Why? Because as soon as you put effort into your spiritual path, your karma is automatically reduced, your spiritual timing can change, as well as destiny. You never want your life based on destiny, timing, karma, and nature. It means you've given your power to these factors to let them influence your life. It means you accept life as it is and you don't want to change it. When you put in effort to understand spirituality, to practice spiritual techniques, to meditate, do yoga, do mantras, do breathing techniques, etc., your life begins to shift. As your life shifts towards a spiritual direction, you can begin to live a life where spirituality is integrated into all aspects of your everyday life. Remember, spirituality is not separate from you. It is you.

As you begin to awaken, you will feel different from the rest of the world. You will see the world with different eyes and begin to change your perspective, attitude, thoughts, and the way you speak and act. Your family and friends may begin to see you changing and might be happy for you or might be afraid for you. It is sad, but not many people like to see their loved one grow spiritually and awaken. They might even consider the spiritual one as "crazy." The reason is because the spiritual person is no longer controlled by societal norms, masks, labels, ideologies, beliefs, culture, and other embedded ideas in the mind. And when someone doesn't live their life according to societal, family or friend's expectations they are considered "weird." I share this truth with you because it is important for you to know and be aware.

When I began to awaken, my dad and other family members did not like it. My friends thought I was putting up a wall because I didn't want to hang out with them anymore, and I wanted to be by myself. They felt I wasn't the same anymore, that I was becoming lost, and losing myself. They blamed my spirituality for it and my "Indian teacher," as if it were his fault that I was changing. In reality, I wasn't changing. I was shedding my layers to discover who I really was. I was inspired by myself to know myself. I wanted freedom. Society, family, and friends could not provide me with that, nor will they ever. Freedom belongs to me. It is up to me to go and find it.

I read a quote once that said, "When someone says, 'you've changed' it simply means you've stopped living your life their way," and found this statement to be so true. You've lived your life based on other's definitions, labels, and expectations of you. When you grow spiritually and awaken, you live your life according to you. True freedom means to fully shine, be yourself, express yourself, with no one or any chains holding you back.

As you grow and you wish others to respect your journey and transformation, you must also pay the same respect to them. Don't judge others for not being on the path, or not understanding you, or even caring about your spirituality. When it is their time to grow and blossom, they will. Remember, you cannot force anyone to change, nor can you force anyone to understand you. Live your life for yourself, don't wait for others to accept your new spiritual life, don't wait for their approval or validation. If you wait for others, you will wait forever. Remember, you need to be strong. You need to love yourself, believe in yourself, validate yourself, appreciate yourself, and approve yourself—that is what matters the most. It's your head that hits the pillow at night time. You have to live with yourself. Do what feels right for you. Don't live for others. Live for yourself. If others call you selfish, so be it. It's about time you put yourself first!

I understand that on your spiritual journey you might begin to feel alone. No one understands you. No one supports you. No one truly gets what you are doing and why spirituality means so much to you. That is why it is important to find other like-minded spiritual people and surround yourself with such friends. When guests come to Siddhayatan Spiritual Retreat, they are so excited to meet others who are the same age, have gone through similar experiences, are trying to be spiritual and live in the world at the same time, and that their challenges are similar. When they meet new friends and gain that support, they don't feel "abnormal" anymore, and most important, they do not feel alone. They appreciate the support.

I know what it is like to appear like the crazy and weird one. I know what it feels like to be misunderstood and alone. I know what it feels like to try to explain spirituality to your loved ones because you want them to be inspired too. I know what it is like to have hope in your friends and family for them to change, and to be continually let down. I know the fear of "coming out of the closet" and telling your family you are no longer religious, but spiritual. I know what it is like to lose family and friends, whom you love dearly, in order to find yourself. I know what it is like to be the awkward and different one—the vegetarian, the spiritual one. I know what it is like to feel hurt, saddened, and full of pain, knowing that you want to be spiritual and make a difference in the world, yet no one understands or supports you. I know it. I get it. I understand it. You might go through similar experiences. Always remember, if any of this comes up, why finding yourself means so much to you. What freedom means. What living a life full of purpose means. What living a meaningful life means to you. Why you want to be spiritual. Why you want to remove your pain, suffering, and karma. When you remember who you are, the path, your effort, and the positive results thus far, you will continue bravely, courageously, and with soul strength on your spiritual journey. Remember, you are not alone. There are other seekers, like myself, who are like you. Sometimes you have to lose everything to gain everything.

What has helped me on my spiritual journey is having a spiritual master guide me. *Guru* in Sanskrit means "one who dispels darkness." I always see the guru, or spiritual teacher, as a flashlight. You must walk into the dark pitch-black cave to discover all of the hidden treasures. The guru is your flashlight. They shine light on areas of the cave to help you, but it is still your journey. You still have to walk. You still have to discover. You have to do all the digging and the handwork. They are there to guide you, not to do everything for you, and not to save you. It's your battle, but they can train you and show you the process. You only value things when you work hard for them. If something is easy, you won't value it. When you achieve enlightenment and liberation, you will value it, because you knew how long it took to get there and what was required of you. The spiritual teacher is your trainer.

The path to Enlightenment is the ultimate test of the soul. The Olympics is nothing compared to Enlightenment. Winning a war is nothing. Conquering your inner enemies and dissolving all karma is the biggest win of all. Win over yourself and then you realize the real you, soul, is the ultimate prize. You become a *Jina*—the victorious one. You have crossed the ocean of suffering, conquered yourself, and are now free.

If you need help on your spiritual journey, know that Acharya Shree, myself, and all other teachers at Siddhayatan are here for you. Make effort to be in contact and to meet us. Direct guidance is very helpful on your journey. If it wasn't for the direct guidance of Acharya Shree, I know I wouldn't be where I am at today. I remember I asked Acharya Shree once, "If I didn't meet you, would I have still reached Enlightenment in this life?" "No, it would have taken many, many lifetimes. When you have the guidance of a master, it saves you from wasting even more time in the cycle of birth and death. A master knows you. A master will know how to help you become liberated. Always value the master and never take him or her for granted." Seek guidance from a true master or spiritual teacher. They are the real flashlights for your spiritual journey. Be wise who you entrust your path with. There are many out there who appear spiritual, wise, and claim to be enlightened, so be cautious. True enlightenment is rare.

I know Acharya Shree is a truly enlightened one. He is not seeking followers. He always says, "I'm not here to teach. I'm here to share. I am not here to collect followers. I am here to make masters." I wouldn't have continued learning from Acharya Shree if I thought he was not real. His wisdom comes from his soul. He doesn't rely on books. He knows the path, because he has walked it. He knows my soul and has helped my soul grow tremendously. I didn't stick around for over eleven years without experiencing transformation, self-realization, and tasting my soul. What I used to dream about achieving spiritually, regarding soul and meditation, I have already surpassed. I thought it would take me a lifetime to get where I am today. With Acharya Shree's guidance, I have arrived much sooner, with the rest of my life to continue to grow, advance, and make effort to liberate myself. What I have shared with you in this book, comes from my experiences and understanding of Acharya Shree's teachings that have affected and transformed my life. I'm here to pass on the seeds, which he has passed to me. It's time for you to grow. It's time for you to blossom. It's your time.

After these thirty-one days of teachings, techniques, tips and tasks, you now truly have a strong foundation to begin or advance your spiritual journey. What you have learned in thirty-one days, has taken me years to learn, understand, and practice. What you now know and need to practice, is the guidance, teachings, and techniques I wish I'd had when I first started my spiritual journey when I was seventeen. When I first began my journey of self-discovery, all I had was myself, my scattered yet curious mind, and a couple of self-help books, which didn't answer my questions or provide me with soulful solutions. I wish I had had a book that held many spiritual gems to get me started, that explained the teachings, why it was important, the benefits of doing such a practice, explain the actual technique, plus the inspiration to go out and do it. You have everything you need now to begin and advance your spiritual journey.

I encourage you to read this book again and again. The reason is that you will read this book one way and then change and transform. When you reread it, it will be with different eyes and you may learn something more.

Practice. Practice. Practice. In order to liberate your soul, you must put forth effort. You must put effort into removing your clouds, karma, confusion, illusion, ignorance, darkness, pain, and suffering. Your life is in your hands. Practice these techniques. Become nonviolent. Let go and release pain and suffering. Meditate. Practice awareness. Focus. Be non-attached. Recite mantras. Do yoga. Be active in your soul day and night. Live moment to moment. Be still and silent. Activate your chakras. Set up a sacred space. Cleanse your body and soul through fasting. Respect your body. Like and love yourself. Discover and live out your true purpose. Be strong and shine despite any problems that come your way. Be humble. Dissolve your ego. Shed your layers of karma. Take a vow. Practice.

My dear friend and fellow truth seeker, it's your time to shine. It's your time to fly. It's your time to be free. It's your time to awaken. It's your time to realize your true self. It's your time to realize you are love. You are divine. You are pure. You are innocent. In this moment, you can decide to live from soul. Release your past. Release your pain. Release your anger. Release your suffering. Say good-bye to guilt. Say good-bye to resentment. Welcome peace in your heart. Welcome compassion. Welcome love. Welcome forgiveness. Put forth effort daily. Change yourself. Change the world.

Always remember:

Shine Through Wisdom

Believe in yourself. Love yourself. Know yourself.
Because hope for a better world starts with you.

Jai Siddhatma!

# :: ABOUT THE AUTHOR ::

**Sadhvi Siddhali Shree** is the Chief Disciple of living enlightened master Acharya Shree Yogeesh and the first North American Jain monk. She was publicly initiated at the age of 24 in 2008. Pre-monkhood, she deployed to Iraq as an Army Combat Medic Sergeant to help soldiers and local Iraqis medically in times of war. She is the Spiritual Director of Siddhayatan Tirth, a 155 acre spiritual retreat center located near Dallas, Texas. She is the author of *31 Days to a Changed You*, a practical guide for personal transformation. In 2013 she released her first piano meditation album *Songs of the Sadhvi*.

As an international speaker she passionately teaches on spirituality, transformation, and personal growth. She is known amongst her peers for her playful, witty yet wise shining spirit.

Meet her at SiddhaliShree.com and Facebook.com/SiddhaliShree.

# :: Additional Resources ::

**Connect with Sadhvi Siddhali Shree**

SiddhaliShree.com

ShineThroughWisdom.com

YouTube.com/SiddhaliShree

Facebook.com/SiddhaliShree

Twitter.com/SiddhaliShree

info@siddhalishree.com


**Siddhayatan Spiritual Retreat Center**

9985 E. Hwy 56, Windom, Tx 75492 USA

http://siddhayatan.org


Order books and audio courses by Sadhvi Siddhali Shree online at http://siddhayatan.org/store.

www.ingramcontent.com/pod-product-compliance
Lightning Source LLC
LaVergne TN
LVHW041212080426
835508LV00011B/923